CW01333785

Therapy Games and Coping Skills for Teens

Go from Stressed to Self-Assured with 200 Fun Activities and a Workbook for Lasting Calm and Confidence

© Copyright 2025 – All rights reserved.

The content contained within this book may not be reproduced, duplicated, or transmitted without direct written permission from the author or the publisher.

Under no circumstances will any blame or legal responsibility be held against the publisher or author for any damages, reparation, or monetary loss due to the information contained within this book, either directly or indirectly.

Legal Notice:

This book is copyright-protected. It is only for personal use. You cannot amend, distribute, sell, use, quote, or paraphrase any part of the content within this book without the consent of the author or publisher.

Disclaimer Notice:

Please note the information contained within this document is for educational and entertainment purposes only. All effort has been executed to present accurate, up-to-date, reliable, and complete information. No warranties of any kind are declared or implied. Readers acknowledge that the author is not engaging in the rendering of legal, financial, medical, or professional advice. The content within this book has been derived from various sources. Please consult a licensed professional before attempting any techniques outlined in this book.

By reading this document, the reader agrees that under no circumstances is the author responsible for any losses, direct or indirect, that are incurred as a result of the use of the information contained within this document, including, but not limited to, errors, omissions, or inaccuracies.

Table of Contents

PART 1: THERAPY GAMES FOR TEENS..1
    INTRODUCTION LETTER TO PARENTS 2
    INTRODUCTION LETTER TO TEEN READERS 3
    CHAPTER 1: UNDERSTANDING THE POWER OF
    MINDFULNESS 4
    SECTION 2: EXPRESSING YOUR THOUGHTS 12
    SECTION 3: MANAGING STRESS AND ANXIETY...................................18
    SECTION 4: BUILDING EMOTIONAL RESILIENCE 25
    SECTION 5: CONFIDENCE BOOSTING TECHNIQUES 33
    SECTION 6: CREATING A MINDSET OF GROWTHP............................40
    SECTION 7: BUILDING SOCIAL SKILLS: THE ESSENTIALS 52
    SECTION 8: MEDITATION AND VISUALIZATION 57
    SECTION 9: MIND AND BODY CONNECTION 64
    SECTION 10: SETTING A ROADMAP FOR THE FUTURE 68
    THANK YOU MESSAGE..77
PART 2: COPING SKILLS FOR TEENS 78
    INTRODUCTION LETTER TO PARENTS 79
    INTRODUCTION LETTER TO TEEN READERS 80
    SECTION 1: UNDERSTANDING EMOTIONS: THE WHY,
    WHAT, AND HOW 82
    SECTION 2: THE UPS AND DOWNS OF TEENAGE YEARS 90
    SECTION 3: MINDFULNESS – YOUR EMOTIONAL
    LANDSCAPE 98

SECTION 4: THE POWER OF POSITIVE THINKING 106
SECTION 5: TECHNIQUES FOR STRESS MANAGEMENT 116
SECTION 6: BOUNCING BACK FROM SETBACKS 122
SECTION 7: CREATING HEALTHY RELATIONSHIPS 130
SECTION 8: SOCIAL MEDIA AND MENTAL HEALTH 141
SECTION 9: EMPATHY AND COMPASSION TOWARDS OTHERS 146
SECTION 10: YOUR EMOTIONAL TOOLKIT – A PERSONALIZED PLAN 151
A THANK YOU MESSAGE 159
CHECK OUT ANOTHER BOOK IN THE SERIES 161
REFERENCES 162
IMAGE SOURCES 168

Part 1: Therapy Games for Teens

200 Mindful Activities for Enhanced Coping Skills, Expression, and Self-Worth

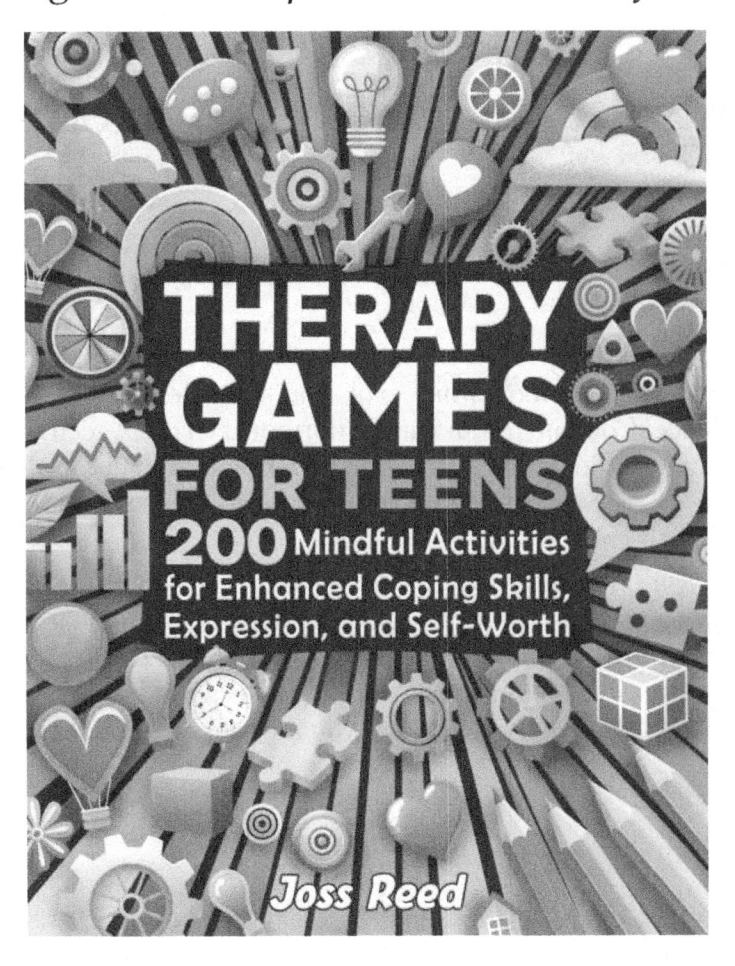

Introduction Letter to Parents

Dear Parents,

Your teenager's mental health and emotional development are important to you – or you wouldn't have picked up this book in the first place.

Teenagers are uniquely vulnerable. At this point in their life, they are looking to you for support while exploring their identity and striving for independence. Combined with natural hormonal changes, teens often face mental health challenges that can follow them into adulthood. If you are reading this book, you care about your teenager's mental health and want to support their growth.

The activities are designed as a resource, not to replace your support, but to complement it. They are also intended to give your teenager the tools they need to support their *own* mental health. We encourage you to actively engage and communicate with your teenager and participate in activities alongside them so they know you are with them on their journey.

Introduction Letter to Teen Readers

Dear Teen,

You have been given this book by somebody you trust. It does not mean you're broken!

We all need help navigating through our lives. Your struggles with school, life, relationships, and friendships are normal. This book is designed to give you tools to help you stay on an even keel, even if your grades aren't what you want them to be or the person you have a crush on won't give you the time of day.

Believe it or not, we've all been there. The activities and tips in this book have been shown to help teenagers deal with everything that, right now, seems like it might be the end of the world. Use this book to help and rely on the trusted adults in your life for advice and support.

Chapter 1: Understanding the Power of Mindfulness

Mindfulness sounds weird, but it's actually a very simple concept. So, let's start by understanding what it is and what it can do for you.

What Is Mindfulness?

Mindfulness is being aware of the moment, yourself, and your surroundings. A lot of the time, we rush from one thing to another without thinking. Think about your typical school day and how you dive from class to class, chat with your friends over lunch, and then rush home or to extra-curricular activities. You might not have time to stop.

Mindfulness is all about stopping, even if it's only for a moment, and checking in with yourself.

The Benefits of Mindfulness

Think back to the last time you played some kind of sport. If you don't know where the ball is, you can't catch it, right?

So, mindfulness starts by knowing where your personal balls are. You can't fix a problem if you don't know what it is, which also goes for your mental health.

Getting that kind of awareness is not easy, but it's well worth it. Here are some ways mindfulness can make your life better:

- It makes you less anxious. Think about how much easier exams and tests would be if you worried less about them.
- It increases your self-awareness, helping you be a better person.
- It increases your awareness of your emotions, letting you regulate them better.
- It helps you sleep better.
- It can increase your performance in sports by reducing stress and performance anxiety.
- It improves relationships by giving you better control over emotions and behaviors that can alienate your friends and family.

Mindfulness can help every single part of your life. It's not just for people who are having problems. It's for everyone. Lots of famous people swear by mindfulness meditation to help their lives and make them more successful: Emma Watson, Lady Gaga, Katy Perry, Miley Cyrus, and LeBron James are a few examples. We bet your favorite celebrity does it, too.

Mindfulness Games

Here are some exercises to improve your mindfulness:

1. Basic Walking Meditation

Walking meditation can help you improve your mindfulness.[1]

a. Choose a space 10 to 20 feet long or a quiet path.

   b. Walk along the space or the path, turning at the end.

   c. Focus entirely on the act of walking, on the movements that help you stay balanced.

2. **Body Scan Meditation**

   a. Lie on your back with your legs extended, arms at your side, palms up.

   b. Focus your attention on each part of your body, from your toes to your head.

   c. Be aware of sensations, emotions, or thoughts associated with each part.

3. **Sitting Meditation**

   a. Sit with your back straight, feet on the floor, and hands in your lap. Choose a chair that is not too comfortable or too uncomfortable.

   b. Breathe through your nose.

   c. Make a note of each sensation or thought that interrupts you, then return to your breath.

4. **Paced Breathing to Reduce Anxiety**

   a. Inhale for four counts.

   b. Exhale for seven counts.

5. **Progressive Muscle Relaxation**

   a. Focus on a body part and then tense and relax muscles. You can do your shoulders, hands, etc.

6. **5-4-3-2-1**

This is an awesome grounding exercise. Pay attention and mention out loud or internally:

   a. Five things you can see

   b. Four sensations you can feel

   c. Three sounds you can hear

   d. Two things you can smell

   e. One thing you can taste.

7. Personality Tree

Personality Tree

a. Write your values on the roots

b. Write your strengths on the trunk

c. Write your goals on the branches.

8. Raisin Meditation

a. Take a raisin (or some other small fruit)

b. Note the color

c. Feel the texture

d. Smell the raisin

e. Put the raisin in your mouth and savor the taste

f. Eat the raisin

9. Use STOP

a. **S**tand up and breathe.

b. **T**une into your body.

c. **O**bserve what your body is telling you.

d. **P**ossible: What is possible here?

10. Yawn and Stretch

Consciously yawning and stretching help you be more aware of your body.

Yawning and stretching can make you more aware of your body.[2]

11. Be Your Own Best Friend

Tell yourself the things you would tell a friend in your situation. This stops negative self-talk.

12. Mindful Cleaning

Nobody likes cleaning their messy room. But if you turn it into a mindfulness activity, it will help your mood, and it will actually get done!

13. Dancing

    a. Put on a favorite song.

    b. Dance to it with your eyes closed. Focus only on the music and how you are moving.

Dancing can help with mindfulness.[3]

14. Mantras
A mantra is simply a word or short phrase.
- a. Choose something aspirational, such as "peace" or "calm."
- b. Think about that word/mantra with each breath.

15. Box Breathing

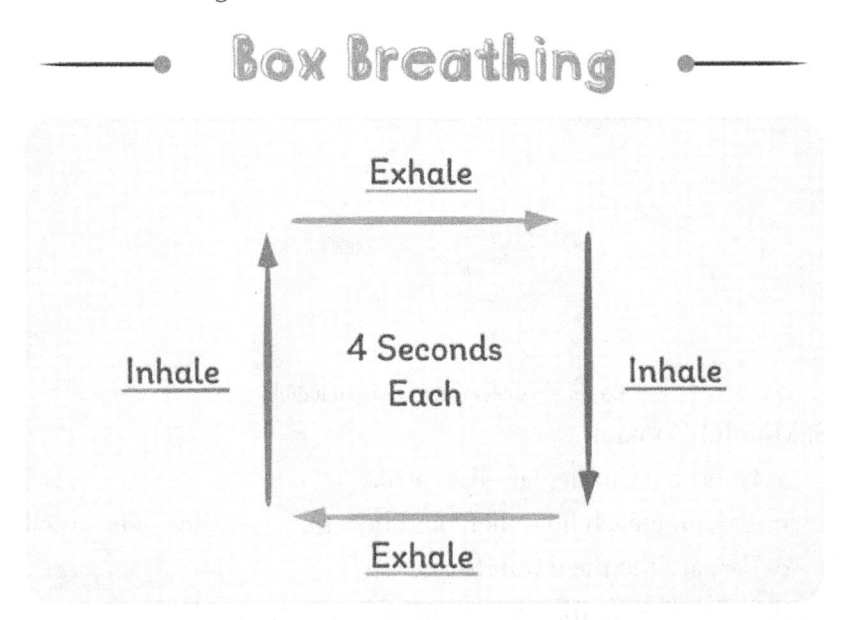

Box Breathing

Exhale · Inhale · 4 Seconds Each · Inhale · Exhale

- a. Inhale and envision drawing one side of a box.
- b. Exhale and do the second side.
- c. Inhale for the third side.
- d. Exhale for the fourth side.
- e. Repeat as needed.

16. Safari
- a. Take a walk in a park or the woods.
- b. Try to find all the animals, insects, and plants you can.

This is great to do with siblings or parents. Leave your phone at home.

17. Blowing Bubbles
- a. Get some bubble solution at the dollar store, or make it with dish soap and water.
- b. Blow bubbles and watch them.

Blowing bubbles can improve mindfulness.[4]

18. Mindful Cooking

    a. Choose a simple, familiar meal.

    b. Examine each ingredient and how they look, feel, and smell.

    c. Prepare the meal with focus.

    d. Eat the meal, focusing on it, with no phone or TV.

19. Three Good Things

    a. Acknowledge your feelings.

    b. Name three good things happening in your life. Your parents can help with this one.

20. Puzzles

Doing your favorite crossword puzzle, Sudoku, etc., without interruptions is a great mindfulness exercise.

Puzzles

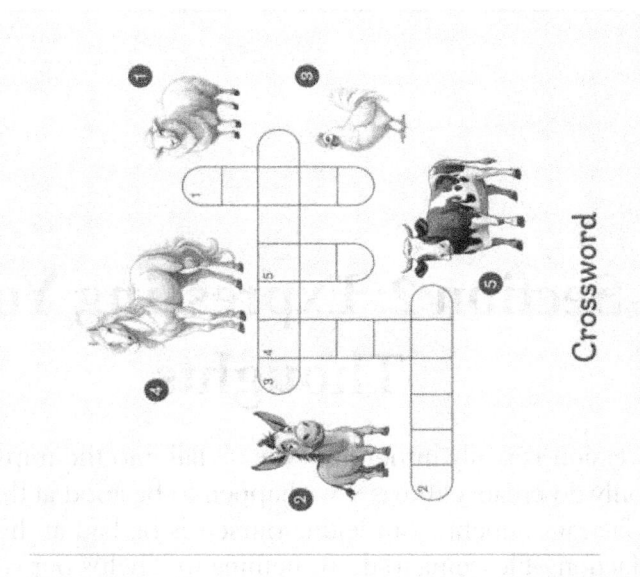

Crossword

Sudoku

		9	5		8			1
	5	6	9		1		7	
			3				2	5
1		2		3		7		
	7		6	3			1	
8	6	1		4				3
9	2			6				
1	4	7	8	2			2	
3			6	9		2		

Section 2: Expressing Your Thoughts

Self-expression is really important! We all fall into the trap of thinking we should only do creative things if we happen to be good at them. That's not true. In fact, we benefit from letting ourselves be bad at things. That said, the satisfaction of learning to do something well helps our confidence.

There are a variety of creative mediums you can use, which include:

- Journaling
- Art
- Fiction
- Crafting
- Music
- Poetry

Different mediums use different parts of your brain. You will probably find one or two that help you more than others, so try them all and see what helps.

How Creativity Works with Mindfulness

Mindfulness and creativity go together. Art therapy, for example, helps people with depression and anxiety. At the same time, mindfulness helps you be more creative. Being creative then helps you express yourself, become more aware of your emotions, and develop a skill. Also, it's a lot of fun.

Creative Exercises

Here are some creative exercises that will help you be more mindful and happier.

21. Painting Kindness Stones
    a. Take a large pebble.
    b. Paint a design on it.
    c. Add an affirmative word such as "Hope," "Love," or "Family." You could also do pictures of your pets or the name of a friend – or your own name.

22. **Adult Coloring Books.** Coloring is *not* just for little kids. Staying within the lines requires focus, and you can pick colors to be realistic...or not.

23. **Journaling.** Journaling can be writing, art, or both. You could even try a photo journal. It helps you be aware of all that's happening in your life.

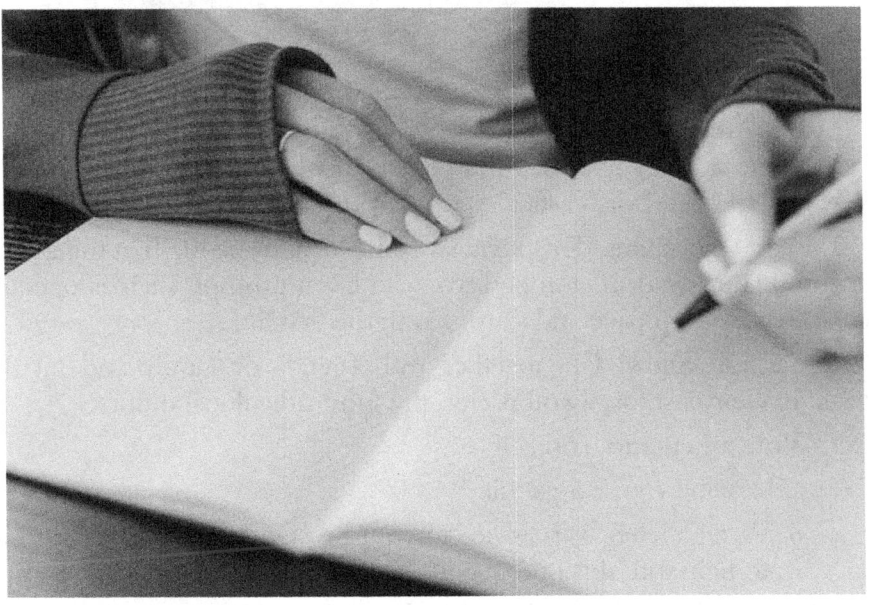

Journaling can help you become more aware of what's happening in your life. [5]

24. Poetry Slam
    a. Write a poem that expresses your emotions.
    b. Get together with trusted friends.
    c. Read your poems to each other with as much force as possible.

25. Playlists

Years ago, people used to make:" mix tapes." Now, we make *playlists*.

>   a. Come up with a mood you want to create or a story you want to tell
>
>   b. Put together music that supports that mood, using tracks you own or your favorite streaming service

Creating playlists depending on your mood can help you express your thoughts.[6]

26. **Write a Story from a Prompt.** Use a word or image as a starting point, such as "ogre" or "castle."

27. **Free Association.** This means writing or drawing the first things that come into your head. If stumped, you can use a prompt, such as opening a book to a random page and starting with the first line.

28. **Fashion Show!** Get together with friends or family and hit the catwalk in your best (or, if you prefer, the most ridiculous) outfit.

29. Write a Letter to Yourself

>   a. Imagine you're an adult.
>
>   b. Write a letter with advice to your present self. Get your parents to help with this one.

30. Collage Yourself. (*Or Mood Board, if You Prefer.*)

>   a. Focus on your values and the things you find important.
>
>   b. Collect images that show what they mean to you.

31. **Write a Song.** Songwriting is a great way to express yourself as it brings together music and poetry.

Songwriting can help you express yourself.[7]

32. Develop Your Photography Skills. You already have a phone (probably), and going out and taking pictures of things in your neighborhood is a lot of fun. It also helps you notice what you might not have otherwise seen.

33. Blackout Poetry (Also Called "Found Word Poetry")

    a. Take a page of a book or newspaper (you can make a photocopy).

    b. Blank out words until what's left forms a poem.

34. Origami. The ancient art of paper folding. You can find lots of patterns online to make various creatures and images.

Origami has many patterns.[8]

35. Mandalas. Another ancient art. Drawing a mandala in sand, if available, or on paper requires a lot of focus and relaxation.

Examples Of Mandalas

A

B

C

36. **Bag Self-Portrait**
   a. Get a paper bag.
   b. Draw a self-portrait on the outside, which can be accurate or stylized.
   c. Fill the bag with items that represent you.

37. **Draw Yourself as a Warrior.** Or a scientist, astronaut, superhero, or whatever represents personal strength to you. This can help you feel stronger.

38. **Dress as a Warrior.** Making your own costume to wear can be incredibly fulfilling, and you don't need to be able to sew. You can put it together from your wardrobe or visit thrift stores.

39. **Draw or Write about Things That Scare You.** This can help you feel as if you're in control of the monsters.

40. **Write a Fairy Tale about Yourself, with a Happy Ending That Is Personal to You**

Section 3: Managing Stress and Anxiety

We all get stressed and anxious. Being a teenager can be really stressful. You have to worry about your grades, friendships, and position on a sports team. Sometimes, it feels like so many expectations are placed on you that you will never meet all of them!

Don't worry! It's normal to be stressed. In the U.S., three-quarters of high school students experience boredom, anger, fear, or stress in school. The same number are "often or always" stressed by their schoolwork.

We can't always get rid of the causes of our stress, but managing it better can help us stay healthy. If you are really stressed, there's no shame in seeking professional help. A good therapist can give you even more tools to help with your stress.

Benefits of Improved Stress Management

Managing your stress better can help you:
- Have better relationships
- Keep up with your responsibilities
- Sleep better
- Stay healthy
- Be happier overall

There are many ways to manage your stress, including going on walks in nature, talking it out with a trusted adult, making time for fun, and writing it down. Mindfulness has been shown to reduce stress and improve self-esteem and overall mental health.

Stress Management Games

Here are some activities that can help reduce your stress.

41. Deep Breathing. Paced breathing (inhale for four counts, exhale for seven counts) can help reduce anxiety in the moment. When we breathe deeply, we actually affect our body in ways that reduce stress.

42. Put Your Hands in Water
- a. Fill a bowl or go to a stream.
- b. Put your hands in the water.
- c. Focus on the water's temperature and how it feels on parts of your hand.

Putting your hand in a stream can reduce stress. [9]

43. Hold a Piece of Ice
- a. Get a chunk of ice from the freezer
- b. Hold it until it starts to melt and focus on the sensation changes that it brings.

44. Do Jumping Jacks. Jumping jacks move your entire body and are just tricky enough that they need a lot of focus.

Jumping jacks can help you focus. [10]

45. Recite a Poem, Song, or Book Passage That You Know *Really Well*. The trick here is to focus deeply on it anyway!

46. Practice Self-Kindness. Repeat compassionate phrases to yourself. Tell yourself you are strong and trying hard, and keep saying it until you believe it.

47. Use Cognitive Reframing
    a. Acknowledge your negative thoughts.
    b. Consciously turn them into positive ones. This can be hard, so don't be afraid to get help.

48. Keep a Mood Tracker
    a. Design a mood tracker that reflects your passions.
    b. Track your mood each day and pay attention to what might have affected it.

Keep a Mood Tracker

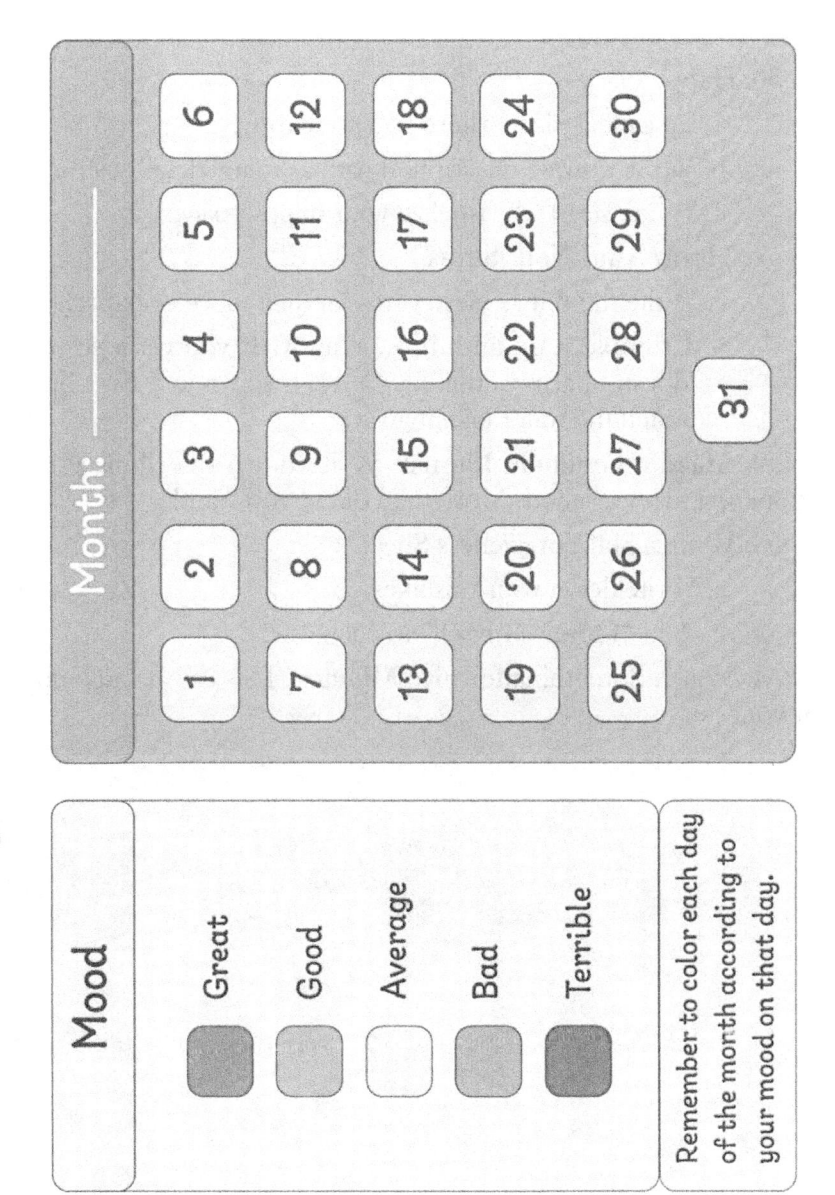

Month: _____

1	2	3	4	5	6
7	8	9	10	11	12
13	14	15	16	17	18
19	20	21	22	23	24
25	26	27	28	29	30
31

Mood

- ☐ Great
- ☐ Good
- ☐ Average
- ☐ Bad
- ☐ Terrible

Remember to color each day of the month according to your mood on that day.

49. **Anchor Breathing**
   a. Imagine that you are in a place you find relaxing, such as a boat on the ocean or deep in the woods.
   b. Breathe deeply.
50. **Happy Place**
   a. Imagine a place where you are happy.
   b. Write down a description with as many details as possible.
   c. When stressed, visualize your happy space.
51. **Throw Away Your Stress**
   a. Write the things bothering you on a piece of paper.
   b. Crumple it up and throw it away. If you use rice paper (which doesn't harm wildlife), you can throw it in a river or stream and watch the water take it away.
52. **Make a Gratitude Journal.** Write down one thing every day that happened that was good. More than one if you want!
53. **Write a Self-Forgiveness Sheet**
   a. Write down your mistakes
   b. Add "I forgive myself" to each one.
54. **Watch Something for Five Minutes.** This can be a cloud, an insect, or your pet.

Watching clouds can relieve your stress. "

55. Write an Affirmation List
   - a. Write down positive affirmations such as "I am strong," "This will work out," "I can be patient."
   - b. Read your affirmation list when you feel stressed.

56. Fog the Mirror
   - a. Hold your hand up in front of your mouth.
   - b. Exhale as if deliberately fogging a mirror, making your breath audible.

57. Find a Touchstone
   - a. Go to a natural place.
   - b. Collect a rock, leaf, pine cone, or similar object.
   - c. Touch or look at your touchstone when you feel stressed.

58. Surf Your Worries
   - a. Think of a recent event that made you stressed and worried.
   - b. Let the anxiety rise, and observe your sensations.
   - c. Let the emotional wave crash over you.

59. The Big Shrug

   When tense, our shoulders creep upwards.
   1. Sit down.
   2. Close your eyes.
   3. Tighten your shoulders up to your ears.
   4. Count to five.
   5. Drop your shoulders as low as you can.

   Repeat five times.

60. Thought Flowing
   - a. Sit down.
   - b. Imagine your thoughts are leaves in a stream or clouds floating past.
   - c. Observe each thought and then let it go.

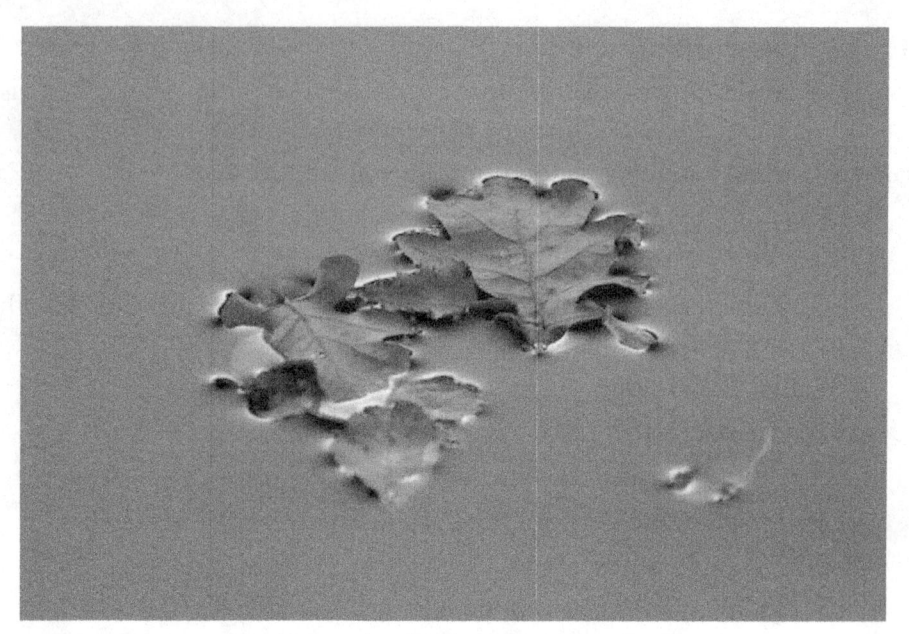

Imagine your thoughts floating down a stream. [12]

Section 4: Building Emotional Resilience

Emotional resilience gets a bad rap. A lot of people think that it means not feeling emotions. This is not true! In fact, the last thing you want to do is try to stop feeling an emotion. When you suppress a negative emotion, such as anger, all you do is build up pressure that will eventually explode.

Instead, emotional resilience is coping with your emotions. Anger, fear, disappointment, etc., are all perfectly natural. However, if we let them control us, we have problems. Failing to control anger, for example, can alienate people and even get you into trouble with the police. Failing to control fear means you won't do things that get you outside your comfort zone and help you grow. Emotional resilience also gives you better self-esteem and vice versa.

How to Build Emotional Resilience

You can't build emotional resilience overnight, and you shouldn't try. It's an ongoing process that you will be working on your entire life. You've seen adults fail to control their temper or get upset about a small disappointment, right? We all have setbacks, and they're part of life. That includes the ones you're learning to deal with *and* setbacks while dealing with them.

Resilience is about growing and adapting to the challenges you face every day.

Emotional Resilience Exercises

Some exercises to improve emotional resilience:

61. Create Your Own Support Circle. This would be family members and friends you can rely on and trust. It might include peers and adults, a trusted teacher, an older mentor, etc.

Create Your Own Support Circle

62. **Practice Gratitude**
    a. Write down a list of things you are grateful for, from the big ones (such as having a home) to the little things that happen every day.
    b. Use your gratitude list to remind you that the bad things aren't so bad.
63. **Challenge Journaling**
    a. Write down the challenges you faced that day.
    b. Write how you responded to them.
    c. Ask yourself how you could have done better and write that down.
64. **Use a Coping Mantra.** Come up with a phrase that helps you break the cycle of worried thoughts – such as, "I'm doing the best I can," "It's going to be okay," or "I am a strong person."
65. **Tell a Different Story**
    a. Write down the event that made you angry or sad.
    b. Rewrite it to have a happier interpretation.
66. **Make a Purpose Star**
    a. Write your name in the center.
    b. Come up with as many purposes as you can and write them on the arms.

Make a Purpose Star

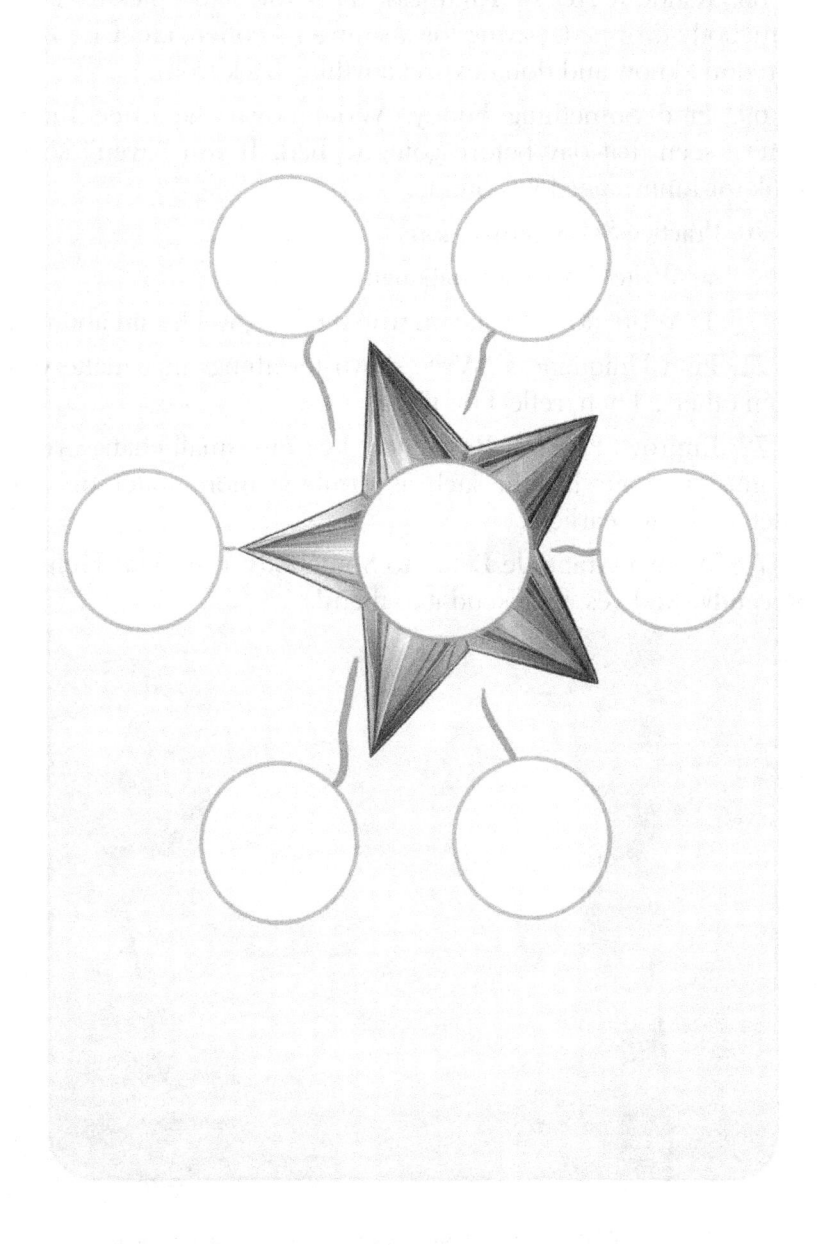

67. Collect Your Strengths
   a. Ask five people close to you to write down what they see as your top strengths.
   b. Look for ones that appear more than once.

68. **Random Act of Kindness.** This might be picking up something somebody dropped, paying for a stranger's coffee, etc. Choose somebody you don't know and don't expect anything back from.

69. **Find Something Funny.** Write down the three funniest things you've seen that day before going to bed. If you haven't seen anything, look for funny anecdotes online.

70. Practice Self-Compassion
   a. Write down the challenging event.
   b. Write down what you would tell a good friend about it.

71. **Find Uniqueness.** Write down the things that make you different from others. Then, reflect on them.

72. **Improve Physical Resilience.** List one small change you can make to improve your health, such as drinking more water or going to bed fifteen minutes earlier.

73. **Write a Gratitude Letter to Somebody Who Has Helped You Out Recently.** And yes, then send it to them!

Writing a letter to someone can help you build resilience. [18]

74. Reframe Thinking
   a. Write down the worst thing that could happen in the challenge you just faced.
   b. Write down the best thing.
   c. Write down what you would tell a friend.

75. **It Could be Worse.** Write down three ways the challenging situation could have been worse. For example, if a friend flaked on you, think, "I could have no friends at all," "They could never come back," or "I could have nobody to talk to about this." Imagining things being worse can help instill gratitude.

76. **Color a Mandala.** Don't think about what colors you use, but use the ones that feel right. This helps you slow down and relax.

77. Write and Destroy a Letter

If you're mad at somebody:
   a. Write them a letter explaining all the reasons you're angry with them.
   b. Delete it, burn it, or shred it. This helps you go through your anger rather than suppressing it. They need never know.

78. *Perfect Is the Enemy of Done* Exercise
   a. Write a story or make a piece of artwork.
   b. Don't edit, revise, or adjust it (don't do this with your homework!)
   c. Show it to somebody.

79. **Name Your Feelings.** List all of the emotions you are experiencing and just say them or write them down. This helps avoid an emotional "flood" that can be hard to deal with.

80. Do a Goal Worksheet
   a. Set goals for the week and the month. Keep them achievable so you feel good when you meet them.
   b. If you fail, write down why, being sure to separate out the external factors you can't control and need to work on not worrying about.

Do a Goal Worksheet

Month _____

Goal: _____

- Week 1 — Goal: _____
- Week 2 — Goal: _____
- Week 3 — Goal: _____
- Week 4 — Goal: _____

Failed? Write down why

Section 5: Confidence Boosting Techniques

Do you feel confident? If your answer is some variant of "No," then that's normal. A lot of teenagers, especially girls, struggle with low self-esteem. Social media and being tied to our phones don't help. Social media encourages us to compare ourselves to our peers or, worse, to celebrities with unrealistic body types. There's also bullying and negative online feedback, such as being called "fat" by people you don't even really know. Or, worse, by people you thought were your friends.

Other things that can impact confidence are being over-scheduled, feeling pushed to be "perfect" by yourself or others, or doing things you don't enjoy and aren't good at because they look good on your college admissions essay.

Building Confidence

Confidence doesn't mean being cocky. In fact, the guy who always seems to be doing everything boldly may be hiding insecurity.

Confidence is very personal, and it involves awareness of your own abilities, trust in them, confidence in your body, etc. It takes time to build confidence, and it's a personal journey that's different for everyone. You don't need to feel jealous of someone with more confidence than you (especially as comparing yourself to others is a great way to *lose* confidence).

Instead, always compare yourself to yourself and look at where you were a few months ago for inspiration.

Confidence Building Techniques

Here are some easy techniques that can help you build confidence:

81. Power Posing

Power posing can help you boost your confidence.

For a few minutes daily, adopt a pose that feels powerful to you. Maybe put your hands on your hips like Wonder Woman or reach up to the sky to make yourself bigger.

82. Positive Self-Talk

Take some time to tell yourself how wonderful you are. If you feel worthless, tell yourself you are worthy. If you feel unloved, remind yourself of the people who love you.

83. Skill Building

Taking up a new hobby and being a beginner can actually be a great confidence booster! We learn more quickly when learning something new, which always feels like an achievement.

Taking up a new hobby, like playing an instrument, can boost your confidence.[14]

84. Goal Setting

Set achievable goals and then reward yourself when you meet them. You may want to work with your parents on this. For example, they can help you come up with rewards. Always set goals that are within your control. "I will get an A in chemistry" is not within your control. "I will hand in all of my chemistry homework on time" is a more reasonable goal.

85. Keep a Compliment Journal

a. Whenever anyone says anything good about you, put it in the journal.

b. When you feel like you can't do anything, reread those past compliments.

86. Self-Portrait Exercise

a. Sketch a self-portrait.

b. Tell yourself how wonderful it looks.

87. Core Belief Exercise

a. Write down three negative core beliefs you have about yourself, such as "I am not attractive" or "I am not smart."

b. Come up with reasons why they aren't true. Or have your parents or a good friend or both tell you why they aren't true.

Core Belief Exercise

Negative core beliefs	Reasons why they aren't true

88. **Positive Word of the Day.** Each day, write down a positive word that describes something you did that day, such as "Helpful," "Kind," or "Victorious."

89. **Mirror Exercise**
    a. Stand in front of the mirror.
    b. Come up with three things you find beautiful about yourself.

Talking to yourself in the mirror can help you see what you like about yourself. [15]

90. **Give Yourself a Certificate.** When you achieve something, award yourself a certificate for the achievement. Maybe it's a better grade than expected or being helpful to a friend.

91. **Play a Cooperative Board Game with Your Friends.** Cooperative board games encourage social interaction and reduce competition.

92. **Do a Self-Appreciation Project**
    a. Print out or draw the body template.
    b. Write all the good things about yourself you can think of inside the template.
    c. Have your friends and family write all the good things they notice *outside* the template.
    d. Put it somewhere you can see it.

A Self-Appreciation Project

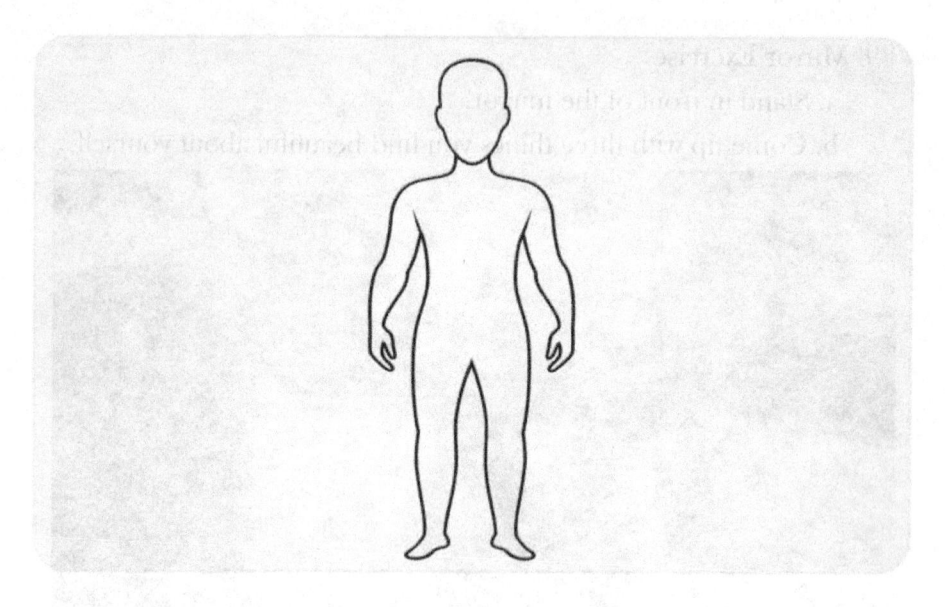

93. Build a Wall of Fame

   a. Get a large corkboard.

   b. Hang it in your room.

   c. Attach proof of your accomplishments. This might include a list of your grades, a medal or certificate you run in sports, a printout of a note of praise, and your name badge from volunteering. Put it where you can easily see it while doing tasks such as homework.

94. Create a Mental Highlight Reel

   a. Visualize the times you experience success.

   b. Rerun the "reel" in your mind when feeling incompetent or lacking confidence.

95. Do Something You Are Afraid to Do. This shouldn't be something actually dangerous but think of things like approaching somebody at school who intimidates you, doing a task you aren't sure you can achieve, etc.

96. Write and Share a Story or Poem. Read a poem to your friends. Maybe enter a writing contest for teenagers.

97. Do a Social Media Purge. Go through your "friends" list and remove anyone who doesn't make you feel good about yourself.

98. Make a Book of Mistakes

    a. List your mistakes

    b. Add what you will do differently next time. If you can't think of anything, seek help from somebody you trust.

    c. Mark any "mistakes" you and your friends think came from external factors.

99. Play the Filter Game.

    a. Take photos and videos.

    b. Do silly things with them. This will remind you that perfect images on the internet or in a movie were probably altered.

100. Make a Photo Book or Scrapbook Showcasing Your Passions, Interests, and the People Most Valuable to You. Feel Free to Include Pets!

Creating a scrapbook will help you see your passions and interests more clearly. [16]

Section 6: Creating a Mindset of Growth

Think of all the adults in your life. Some of them seem stuck where they are and stuck in "can't." Others are constantly learning and taking up new hobbies at the age of 70. The first set has a fixed mindset, and the second set has a growth mindset.

Having a growth mindset means acknowledging that you will never stop learning, growing, and changing. It also means understanding that this is a good thing. Carol Dweck has been researching this for years. According to her, a fixed mindset is the belief that your intellectual ability is fixed and that if you can't do it now, you can never do it. A growth mindset is a belief that you will always be able to develop and improve your abilities.

You can probably work out which is better.

Developing a Growth Mindset

A growth mindset means seeing setbacks as temporary, learning from your mistakes (and other people's), and valuing process over outcome. For example, a fixed mindset might lead to you judging yourself by your grades, which might be affected by your mood the day you took a test, your teacher's mood the day he graded it, or how tough the teacher is. A growth mindset judges by how you achieved those grades and what you learned.

For example, "I can't draw" is an example of a fixed mindset. The alternative is, "I want to be able to draw; how do I get there?" This doesn't mean you should feel as if you have to work on things you don't want to do or don't support your goals.

Growth Mindset Exercises

101. Make and Decorate Growth Posters
    a. Take a large sheet of paper.
    b. Write your next goal on it.
    c. Make it pretty with your favorite doodles.
102. The Paper Challenge
    a. Take paper and scissors.
    b. Try to duplicate the tricky shape. Don't give up; it's not easy, and you may fail a few times.

The Paper Challenge

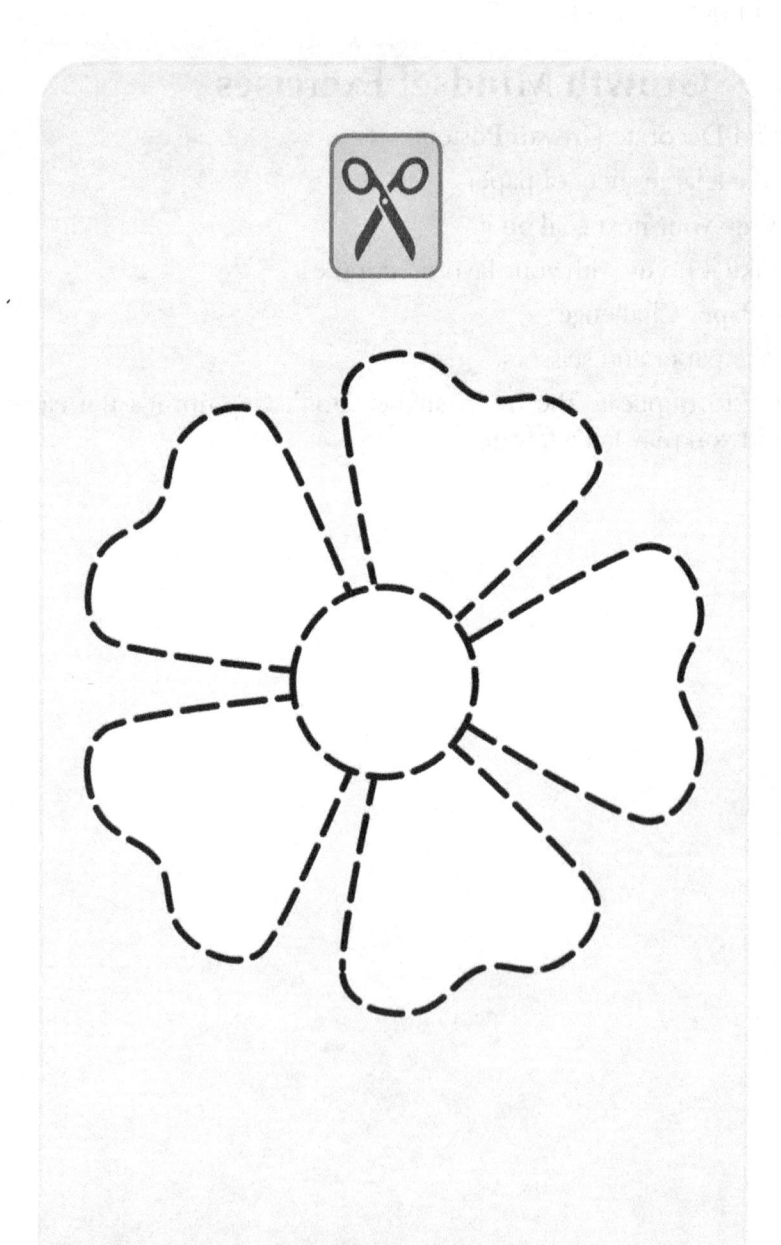

103. Make Growth Mindset Bookmarks. If you read all the time, these are great because you'll be reminded every time you open your book.

    a. Cut a strip of paper or light cardboard.

    b. Write a phrase or Mantra that indicates growth, such as "I can learn to do this."

    c. Add a ribbon to the bottom.

    d. Laminate it if you can.

Make Growth Mindset Bookmarks

> Everything
> is
> hard
> before
> it's
> easy

> Every
> star
> shines
> a little
> differently

> Be
> the change
> that
> you
> wish to
> see
> in
> the world

> This
> may
> take
> some
> time
> but
> don't
> give up

104. **Research a Famous Failure**
   a. Spend some time online and find a famous person who failed hard before they succeeded.
   b. Tell your family or friends about them. Good starting points are Walt Disney, Thomas Edison, and Stephen King.

105. **Read Every Day.** Challenge yourself to read a chapter of a book every day for a month. You will probably want to keep going! It doesn't matter what the book is – but choose one that challenges you!

Reading can help you create a growth mindset. [17]

106. **Make a Vision Board.** A vision board is a collage of your dreams and desires. It's images that represent what you want to do and achieve. Include things you aren't sure you *can* do.
   a. Get a corkboard.
   b. Collect and print out images that represent your desires.
   c. Put it somewhere you can easily see. Or you can do one on your computer.

Make a Vision Board

107. 3-2-1 Exercise

At the end of a day or week, write down the following:

    a. Three things you have learned.

    b. Two things you want to learn.

    c. One question you still have.

108. Keep a Thought Journal. Write down a thought every day that reflects your attitude toward learning. You can spot when you are slipping into a fixed mindset. Then, take those fixed mindset thoughts and change them into growth mindset thoughts!

109. Make a Memory Jar

    a. Take a decent-sized jar.

    b. Every time you achieve something, write it on a slip of paper, then put it in the jar.

    c. Each week, open the jar and read through your accomplishments.

Filling up a memory jar can give you a sense of accomplishment. [18]

110. **Success Iceberg Exercise**
   a. Write a goal at the top.
   b. Write your failures and setbacks below the water line.
   c. When you succeed, write that above the water line at the top.
   d. Keep it as a reminder that you will almost always fail multiple times before succeeding.

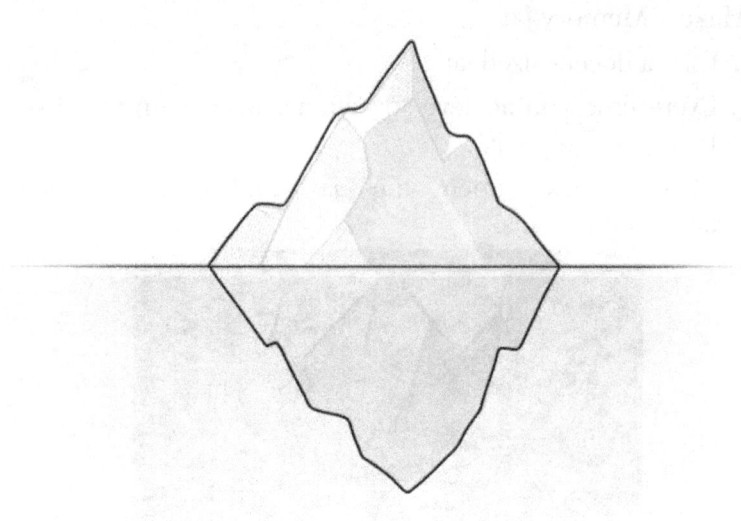

——● Success Iceberg Exercise ●——

111. **Write a Success List**
   a. Write down different ways to achieve success.
   b. Add different definitions of success (hint: It's not always making the most money). This is even more fun if you brainstorm it with somebody else.

112. **Use the "Brains Get Stronger" Mantra.** Repeat it to yourself a few times. Your brain is actually developing a lot right now, and just like a muscle, if you use it, it gets bigger and better.

113. **Play the Yet Game**
   a. Make a statement such as "I don't know" or "I can't."
   b. Add yet to the end.

114. Flip the Flop
   a. Take a piece of paper.
   b. Write a mistake on one side.
   c. Think of an opportunity that mistake created and write it on the other.

115. **Try a New Thing.** This can be as simple as that video game you've wanted to play but think is too hard for you. Let yourself be a beginner.

116. **Moonshot Goal**
   a. Think of something you really want but are convinced you will never achieve, such as writing a book or getting into your preferred college. Take it as far as you want.
   b. Write it down.
   c. Think of things you can do that will be steps toward your moonshot goal.

117. **Do an Already Learned Worksheet**
   a. Create a worksheet with sections for when you were a baby, a toddler, a child, a teenager, and also an adult.
   b. Write down what you have already learned, and yes, this includes how to walk.
   c. In the adult section, write down things you hope to learn in the future.

Already Learned Worksheet

Age	Baby	Toddler	Child	Teen	Adult
Already Learned					

118. Do Error Analysis
   a. Write down a mistake you made.
   b. Write down why you made the mistake.
   c. Write down how you can keep it from happening again.

119. Analyze a Fictional Character
   a. Take a book you love.
   b. Ask yourself if the protagonist has a fixed or growth mindset.
   c. Ask yourself when they change from one to the other.

120. Research Somebody Else's Success. Don't choose a famous person from a famous family. Look at somebody closer to home to see how they worked for their success.

Section 7: Building Social Skills: The Essentials

Without social skills, you won't succeed in life. You won't be able to succeed in a job. More than that, you won't be able to hold stable relationships. Think about how you get on (or don't) with your peers.

It's easy to think that you are the way you are socially, but remember the last chapter! You can improve your social skills, even if you're shy. It just takes time and practice. You don't have to turn into a bubbly extrovert, but you *can* learn to interact better with others.

What Are Social Skills?

We bandy the phrase social skills around a lot but don't often define it. Here are some examples of social skills:

- **Verbal Communication.** Being able to talk clearly and explain what you want to say.
- **Nonverbal Communication.** Making eye contact and controlling your body language.
- **Active Listening.** Being focused on the person you are talking to.
- **Empathy.** Developing an understanding of what other people are feeling.

Yes, people often start with different aptitudes for these skills, but everyone can improve them.

Games to Improve Social Skills

A lot of the activities in this chapter require more than one person. Enlist a sibling, a friend, another family member, etc. You can play these games with your entire family if you want!

121. Use a Conversation Starter

This doesn't mean the weather. Look online, and you can find lots of lists of conversation starters, but consider things like "What have you achieved lately?" "What do you do to relax?" "What book (or movie or TV show) are you reading/enjoying right now?"

122. Role Play

Put yourself in a scenario and practice it with your friends. You can also use this to practice difficult situations, such as finding out you weren't invited to a party or asking somebody out.

123. Conversation Jenga

    a. Get a game of Jenga.

    b. Write a conversation starter question on each block.

    c. As you play, answer the question on the block.

Conversation Jenga can boost your social skills. [19]

124. Charades

It's a classic, but a game of charades helps you practice nonverbal communication and makes everyone laugh.

125. Emotions Uno

    a. Get an Uno set

    b. Make each color in the game stand for an emotion.

c. At the start of the game, when you play a card, mention a time you felt that emotion.

d. After ten minutes, switch to a way you dealt with the emotion.

126. Do a Debate

Pick a fun topic and challenge each other. Choose topics that don't create actual anger for you, such as which fictional character would win in a fight.

127. Play Ball

This doesn't have to be an organized game, but any kind of team game requires physical and nonverbal communication.

Playing a sport, like basketball, can improve nonverbal communication. [20]

128. Play Devil's Advocate

a. Have a debate.

b. Switch sides, so you have to argue a point with which you don't agree. Choose light-hearted topics for this.

129. Improvised Stories

a. Each chooses three objects.

b. Give them to the player on your right.

c. That player then has to include those objects in a short improvised story that they tell right then.

d. Repeat until everyone has had a turn.

130. **Perspective Photos**
  a. Take your phone and a simple object.
  b. Take pictures of it from your perspective, from an ant's perspective, from a giraffe's perspective. Use editing tools if you want!
  c. Show them to your friends and have them guess the perspective used.

131. **Take an Art or Museum Tour with Your Friends.** Choose some exhibits. Discuss them. If getting together is hard, many museums and galleries do virtual tours, which can be easier.

132. **Social Interaction Observation**
  a. Observe an interaction between two or more people.
  b. Write down what you might have done differently. You can do this at school or use a TV show or movie.

133. **Round-Robin Stories**
  a. Tell one sentence of a story.
  b. The player on your right then tells the next sentence.
  c. Repeat until you have a complete story (or can't stop laughing).

134. **Sing Together.** Singing together encourages cooperation, helps you get empathy, and is a lot of fun.

Singing as a group can be a lot of fun. [21]

135. **Do an Escape Room.** If there's an escape room in your area, go with your friends or family. It's a great way to learn to really work together.

136. **Play Two Truths and a Lie.** Each player says three things about themselves. Two are true, and one is not. The rest of the group has to guess which one is the lie.

137. **Practice Saying No**
>   a. Have a friend pretend to be a really pushy salesperson.
>   b. Keep telling them no.
>   c. Switch roles.

138. **Play Spot the Mistake.** One player talks about a familiar topic but makes three or four deliberate mistakes. The rest of the group has to identify the mistakes. Let everyone have a turn.

139. **The Tossing Game**
>   a. Get a *soft* ball (this is not dodgeball).
>   b. Toss the ball to somebody else and say a word.
>   c. Have them toss the ball to a third person.
>   d. Their "victim" must say a *related* word. For example, if the first player says brick, the second might say house. If you say an unrelated word, you're out.

140. **500 Years Ago.** One person imagines they are a time traveler from 500 years ago. The other has to explain something to them in words they can understand.

Section 8: Meditation and Visualization

People have been meditating for a very long time. As far as we know, meditation first started in India and is described in *Vedic* texts from thousands of years ago. It likely started well before it was written down!

It's come to refer to many techniques, but the overall purpose is still to get in touch with your inner self. Meditation is really good for you. Especially when starting out, you need to make a quiet place to meditate. Set aside a corner of your room that's clutter-free and generally has an even temperature. You can use a seat, get a cushion, and sit on the floor. The most important thing is to have a place where you feel like meditating!

Benefits of Meditation

As mentioned, meditation is really good for your health. In fact, meditation has been shown to:

- Reduce stress and anxiety.
- Improve your mood.
- Help you sleep.
- Reduce pain, such as aching muscles from sports.
- Improve memory and recall.

- Increase efficiency in your brain, meaning you can do things faster.
- Reduce blood pressure and heart rate.
- Improve blood flow to the brain.

Meditation gets even better as you get older, so getting in the habit now sets you up for a long life!

Meditation Techniques

Meditation can be really hard to start with. Don't try to just sit there and empty your mind. That's like trying to empty a bucket resting on its side in a creek; it will just fill up again. Here are some simple techniques to get you going:

141. Body Scan Meditation

Body scan pose.

a. Lie or sit down.

b. Focus on your body, starting with your toes and working up to the head. Focus on each body part and notice all sensations.

142. Guided Visualization

Guided visualization means taking a mental journey. It's great for beginners because you're focusing *on* something specific. Imagine walking along a beach, through the woods, or along a mountain trail.

143. Loving Kindness Meditation

    a. Imagine a close friend or loved one is sitting opposite you

    b. Imagine you are connected to them by a white light between your hearts.

    c. Focus on the feelings you have for them

    d. Say, "May I be well, happy, and peaceful."

    e. Say, "May you be well, happy, and peaceful."

    f. Repeat a few times.

144. Labyrinth Meditation

Your community may have a labyrinth. If not, you can make a small one by setting objects on the ground in a spiral. Walk the labyrinth from the outside to the inside and back, focusing on the sensation of walking. Let your thoughts wash over you.

145. Diaphragm Breathing

A lot of us breathe in our upper chest. Breathing from the belly helps us get more air.

    a. Sit or lie on your back.

    b. Rest your hands on your belly, just below the navel.

    c. Breathe in and focus on swelling your belly like a balloon.

    d. Breathe out and let your belly sink toward your spine.

146. Concentration Meditation

Focusing on a candle flame can help with concentration meditation. [22]

a. Look at an object or listen to a repetitive sound. Candle flames are great (but watch out for your fire safety).

b. Every time your mind wanders, refocus on the chosen object.

147. **Mantra Meditation**

a. Choose a word or sound that includes the classic "ohm."

b. Repeat the word or sound.

148. **Bead or Counting Meditation**

Rosaries can be used for counting meditation.[23]

a. Get a bead necklace.

b. Count the beads and move them through your hands, focusing on them. (Rosaries are a form of bead meditation).

149. **Clean Room Visualization**

a. Imagine that your space is completely clean and free from clutter.

b. Focus on how it feels.

150. **Shower Meditation**

When you take your shower, that's a great opportunity to get in some deep breathing. Focus on how the water feels on your skin or the fragrance of your chosen soap.

151. Yoga

Yoga can help you clear your mind.[34]

You don't necessarily have to take a class; there are a lot of yoga videos out there. Yoga involves conscious postures that help clear your mind and also has the advantage of making you more flexible.

152. Reflection

    a. Read a poem you like.

    b. Then, spend a few minutes simply reflecting on it in silence.

153. Alternate Nostril Breathing

    a. Hold your left nostril down with your left thumb.

    b. Inhale through your right nostril.

    c. Hold your right nostril down with your left index figure.

    d. Hold your breath.

    e. Release the left nostril and exhale.

    f. Change sides and repeat.

154. 100-Breaths Technique

This one's easy. Just count each of your breaths to a hundred. Make sure you only count exhales.

155. Make an Energy Ball
   a. Rub your palms together.
   b. Feel the sensation of tingling and heat.
   c. Pull your hands apart with palms facing together.
   d. Move them closer and further apart and play with that feeling of connection.

156. Sound Bath
This isn't a time to choose your favorite angsty pop song. Instead, choose classical music, ambient sounds, etc. Choose music without vocals. Close your eyes and let yourself exist in the sound.

157. Noting Meditation
This means using an anchor such as a candle or sound but being careful to note all of your stray thoughts. Label each thought as it arises. This can be combined with other techniques.

158. Who Am I Meditation
This means sitting and asking yourself, "Who am I?" without attempting to answer that question. Insights may come from your subconscious.

159. Laughter Meditation

Laughter meditation can relax you. [25]

Laughter is great medicine. In this form of meditation, you intentionally start to laugh.

    a. Take a few deep breaths.

    b. Smile

    c. Laugh for a few minutes

    d. Stop laughing

    e. Sit in silence for a couple of minutes.

160. Forest Bathing

Forest bathing can be done in any natural setting.[26]

You don't need a forest; any natural place will do! This Japanese practice means just going out into a natural setting, turning off your phone, and moving slowly while taking deep breaths.

Section 9: Mind and Body Connection

"It's all in your head." Has anyone ever said this to you when you're not feeling well? Our minds and our bodies are strongly connected. A physical ailment can make us depressed, and stress and depression can make us physically ill.

When we're stressed, our adrenal glands release adrenaline and noradrenaline into our bodies, preparing us to fight, take flight, or freeze. Our bodies also release cortisol. If the "threat" continues, then elevated levels of these hormones cause problems with our immune system and increased inflammation. You're more likely to get a cold if you're stressed.

Taking care of your mind helps you take care of your body. Doctors sometimes refer people to therapists to help with this. Physical health affects our mood...imagine you break your wrist and can't play sports for a while. That's not going to make you happy!

Nurturing Your Mental and Physical Health

A lot of people, especially younger people, think they don't have time for their mental health. You need to make time! Being mentally and physically healthy means you will get tasks done faster (have more free time), get them done better (have better grades), and have a consistently better mood.

Everything in this book is, to some degree, about getting mentally healthier, but now we're going to address it more directly.

Tips for Better Health

Here are some exercises and tips to nurture your mind-body connection and improve your health.

161. Cut down on junk food and treats. Don't give them up altogether; that tends to make you binge. Instead of eating sweets every day, try having designated "Sweetie Days."

162. Switch up your lunch sandwich. If you pack a sandwich for lunch, switch out your white bread for whole-wheat bread. Add tomatoes and lettuce, spinach, or another green.

Eating a sandwich can improve your health. [37]

163. Reduce soda/pop. Don't switch to diet drinks, which have been shown to increase cravings. Go for flavored water instead. Cut out energy drinks; they're really bad for you.

164. Always eat breakfast. People who skip breakfast tend to weigh more than those who don't.

165. Challenge your friends to a jump rope or hula hoop contest. Or some other simple physical activity.

Simple physical activities like using a can slightly improve your health. [28]

166. Have a scavenger hunt on foot or on bikes. This exercises the mind and the body at the same time.

167. Eat fruit instead of candy. The natural sugar in fruit is better for you.

168. Challenge your friends to a step challenge. If you all have phones that can count your steps or fitness bands, you can set a challenge for a period of time, say a week, and see who can do the most steps.

169. Turn the volume down. Keep the volume on your phone to less than 70% of the max if using earphones.

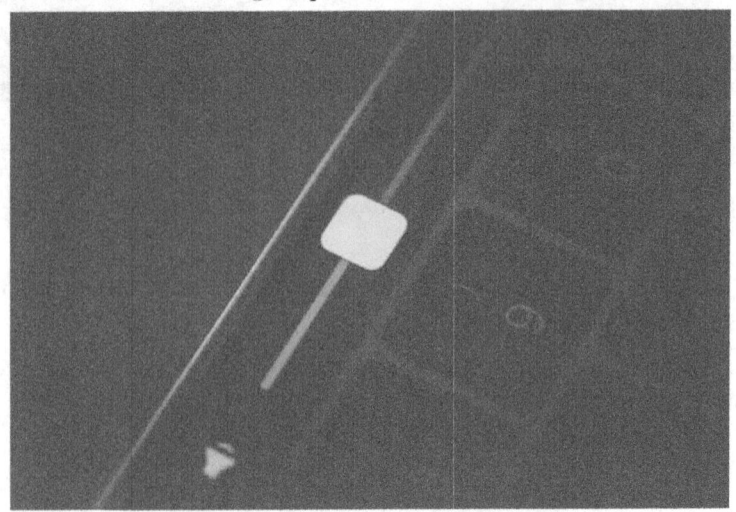

Keep the volume low if using earphones. [29]

170. Keep a regular sleep schedule. Set a bedtime and stick to it, even on weekends.

171. Avoid caffeine in the evenings. This isn't just for teenagers; it's for everyone. Caffeine late at night can keep you from sleeping.

172. Put your phone down an hour before bedtime. Reading a physical book is a great alternative. Screens interfere with your brain, producing sleep hormones. *Turn your phone off at night.*

173. Say no to alcohol and drugs. It's very tempting to try them, especially alcohol, marijuana, and tobacco. However, they're not good for you when your brain is still developing (and not great for adults, either).

174. Practice mindful eating. This means not eating while watching TV or doing homework. Focus on just eating and eat your food slowly.

175. Make fruit water for you and your family. Take a water pitcher and fill it, then add slices of fruit...lemon and lime work well, as does cucumber. Or you can use berries. It's easy and delicious.

176. Improve your posture. A simple exercise that people have been doing for a long time is to walk around with a book on your head. Challenge your friends to see who can do it for the longest.

177. Schedule time for things you love. Put it in writing so you don't forget. If you're doing your obligations all the time, you will experience "burnout" and potentially get ill.

178. Wear sunscreen every time you go outside for an extended period, especially if you have fair skin. Dark-skinned teenagers need it, too, though.

179. Pick up an active hobby or sport. Doing an active thing you love kills two birds with one stone.

Section 10: Setting a Roadmap for the Future

This book is intended as your starting point. You may find some exercises in it more useful than others. Everyone's different; what works for you might not work for others.

Try them; they may spark ideas for other ways to move forward. Ultimately, only you can decide what you most need to stay healthy and happy.

You need a clear direction in life for the future, and hopefully, this book can help you find one. You need goals.

SMART Goals

SMART goals were invented for businesses, but they also work for life! A smart goal is:

- Specific
- Measurable
- Achievable
- Relevant
- Time-bound

You might have an overall goal of starting your own successful business, but that won't work as a SMART goal because it's not time-bound. At the same level, getting straight As is also not a SMART goal because you might not be able to control all the factors that give you your grades, making it impossible.

A really good example of a SMART goal would be "I am going to eat breakfast every day next month." It's specific (tight), measurable (you can check off that you ate breakfast), achievable, relevant (supports your health), and time-bound. After next month, you will have a habit of eating breakfast.

Another example is, "I will read three books this month."

A longer-term SMART goal might be "I'm going to apply to ten colleges." This has a natural deadline. You can't control whether you get in, but you can do things that make it more likely.

You need to be adaptable and reassess your goals. Things change in your life, and things change in you. The career you thought you wanted when you were twelve might not be what you want at sixteen. (Or thirty). Take charge of your future!

Activities to Help You Plan Your Future

Some activities to help you get in the habit of planning and setting goals:

180. Vision Boards

Yes, these have been mentioned before, but that's because they're so good. Set up your vision board with images of what you want to achieve and put it where you can see it.

181. Make a Journal Jar

    a. Brainstorm with your parents or your friends to write down a long list of prompts, such as "What habits would you like to change or develop?" or "Make a bucket list."

    b. Put them in a jar.

    c. Pull one out at intervals and write on it.

182. Make a Wheel of Success

    a. Choose a goal, such as being good enough for the track team.

    b. Identify the performance attributes you need.

    c. Score where you are now.

    d. Score where you need to be. Use it to identify where you need to focus.

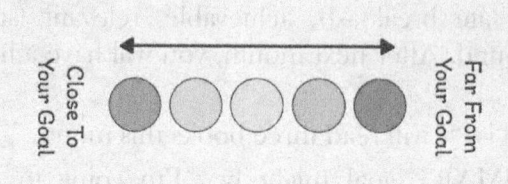

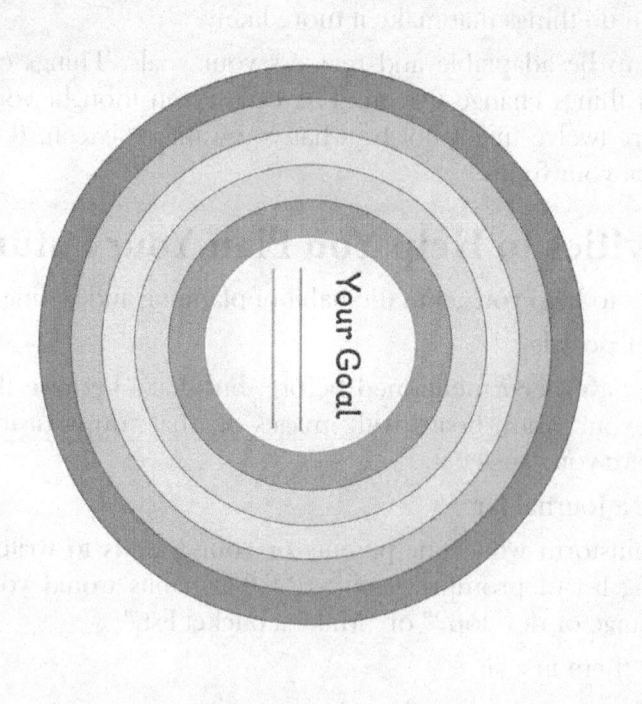

The Wheel of Success

Far From Your Goal ←——→ Close To Your Goal

Your Goal

183. Make a Task List for Each Goal
   a. Break a goal down into smaller tasks
   b. Write them on a piece of paper.
   c. Check them off as they're completed. Be flexible; you may find you need to add or remove tasks.
   d. If you're feeling discouraged, look at what you already did.

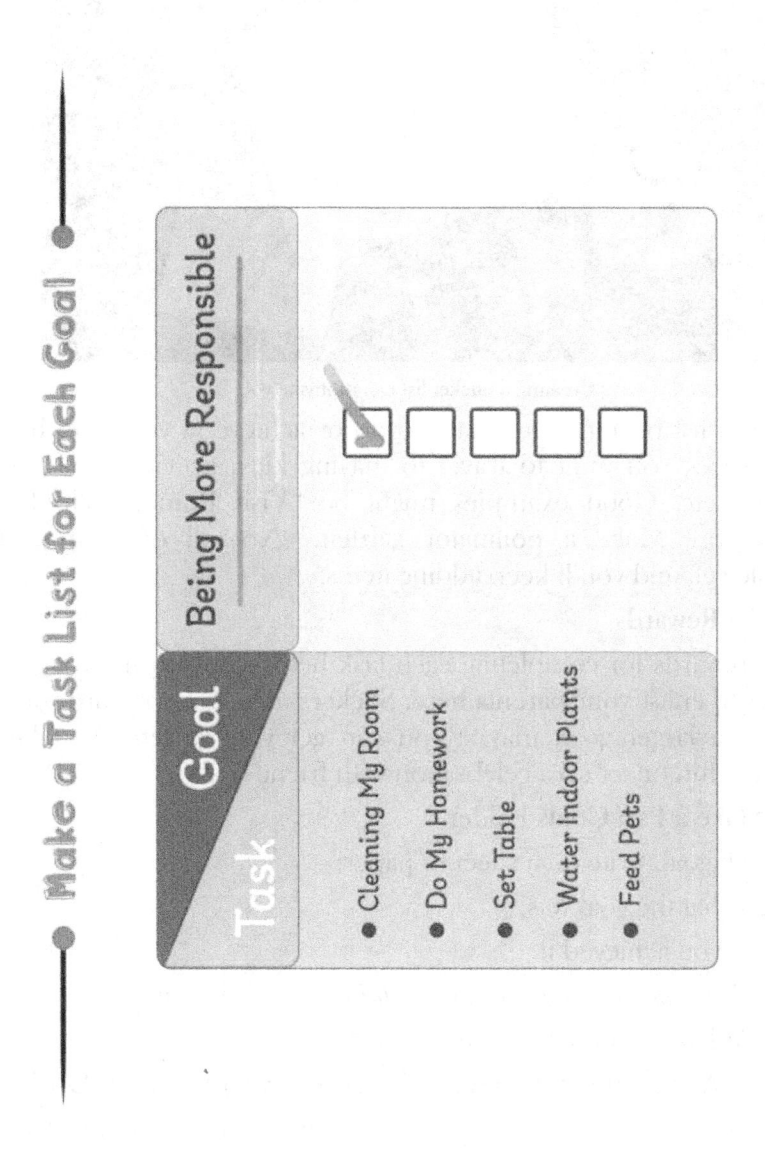

• Make a Task List for Each Goal •

Goal	Task
Being More Responsible	• Cleaning My Room • Do My Homework • Set Table • Water Indoor Plants • Feed Pets

184. **Use Your Goal as a Mantra.** When you wake up, say your most important goal three times.

185. **Make a Bucket List**

Creating a bucket list can motivate you.[30]

This is a list of things you want to do or achieve in your life. It might include places you want to travel to, having kids, activities you want to engage in, etc. Good examples might be "Visit Rome," "Go bungee jumping," or "Make a pollinator garden." Not all of them will be achievable yet, and you'll keep adding items.

186. **Set Rewards**

Small rewards for completing each task help keep you motivated. You may want to enlist your parents here. Stickers are a great reward for small tasks. For a larger goal, maybe you can get your parents to take you somewhere fun or set up a celebration with friends.

187. **Make a Past Goals Folder**

For each goal, write on a sheet of paper:

    a. What the goal was.

    b. If you achieved it.

    c. Why *did* you achieve it/why *didn't* you achieve it?

    d. What the obstacles were.

188. **Set Aside Time for Things That Are *Not* Part of Your Goals**

If you focus on goals all the time, you can get depressed and feel as if you aren't "allowed" to relax and have fun.

189. Record the Process

For example, if you are trying to improve your running time, keep a record of your times. Then, you can look at how they have improved. If your goal is to improve your writing, looking at how bad your journal entries were a year ago can help.

190. Mirror Your Goals

Stick your goal to the bathroom mirror so you see it every time you go in there. If this would cause confusion, another great place is above your bed, where you'll see it when you get up.

191. Journal Your Wishes

    a. Whenever you think or say "I wish," put it in your journal.

    b. Look through your wishes to see if you can turn any of them into goals.

192. Find a Goal Buddy

This doesn't have to be somebody with the same goal, but it helps if it's a friend with a similar goal. If your goal is to work out four times a week, a friend who works with you can help.

193. Ask Your Parents or Your Buddy to Grade You on Your Goals

Strive to reach an A.

194. Set Up a "Goal Club" with Your Friends Where You Share Goals and Encourage Each Other

Don't invite anyone who is prone to criticizing everyone.

195. Clean Your Desk

Keeping your desk clean can declutter your mind. [31]

This might not seem related, but your mind gets cluttered if the space you work in is cluttered. Before doing homework, spend a few minutes removing everything irrelevant.

196. Write an Intentions List

At the start of the day, write down everything you intend to do that day. It feels good to check things off!

197. Make an Eisenhower Matrix

This is a four-square matrix that allows you to prioritize tasks as important, not important, urgent, and not urgent. Remember that fun is important too!

Make an Eisenhower Matrix

Important	Not Important

Urgent	Not Urgent

198. Use a Calendar or Planner

A calendar can help you track your progress.[32]

This helps you track everything you must do by a certain time, such as homework or things you promised a friend.

199. Take Time to Do Nothing

This is the last tip for a reason. We tend to over-schedule our lives. Sometimes, it's good to do absolutely nothing.

200. Fortune Wheel

Get a piece of cardboard paper and draw a circle on it. Divide the circle into sections and write down various goals of yours. Stick a pointer in the middle and design your wheel with colors and stickers to make it fun to use. This fortune wheel of goals can be a fun and stimulating way to choose a goal to work on when you're not sure which goal to work toward first.

Thank You Message

Thank you for buying and reading this book. More than that, thank you for committing to personal growth.

The world needs young people with grit and courage; even taking the first steps toward improving your life proves you have just that! Your future is bright.

This book is a starting point. It's a nudge in the right direction. The rest is up to you. We invite you to stay connected and to share your progress with us and each other.

Thank you for being you!

Part 2: Coping Skills for Teens

A Structured Workbook for Recognizing and Transforming Negative Emotions

Introduction Letter to Parents

Dear Parents/Caregiver,

    Coping Skills For Teens serves as a resource material for you and your teenager. With the help of this book, you can help your teenager develop powerful thinking skills, emotional intelligence, and resilience.

    Raising an adolescent can be difficult, but *so is being one.* It is crucial to support your teen by being a friend and guiding them as they develop emotionally. Start by showing them they are not alone in what may initially seem lonely. Knowing that you care for their emotional and mental health will make them feel safe. Have conversations with them about mental health issues, but don't pressure them into opening up to you, as this might lead to them withdrawing.

    If you struggle with having conversations with your teenager, take it slow. Begin by discussing their interests, spending quality time with them, being candid about your mental challenges as a teenager, and paying attention to what they have to say. Remember to lead by example by modeling emotional intelligence and avoiding actions and words that appear dismissive and nonchalant. Your children will end up emulating your behavior. Your decision to read this book demonstrates your interest in your adolescent's psychological and emotional growth. Thank you for taking this step, and hopefully, this book will serve as a valuable tool in fostering your teenager's mental and emotional well-being.

Introduction Letter to Teen Readers

Dear Teen Readers,

You're growing and changing rapidly, which is a challenging and exciting phase for you. This age of exploration not only changes you physically but also affects you psychologically. You might feel like your emotions are out of your control, you're losing friends, and you're yearning for independence. You should know this is perfectly natural, and you're not alone.

Coping Skills For Teens will guide you through this new phase. With the help of this book, you will be able to understand and manage difficult emotions. These sections provide strategies for enhancing your emotional development and well-being, building healthy relationships, managing stress, and navigating social media. As you read this book, please keep an open mind when it comes to trying new strategies and practicing a healthy lifestyle. And most importantly, don't be afraid to ask for help when needed; you shouldn't expect or pressure yourself to have it all together. You first need to believe that you can become the best version of yourself. Coping Skills For Teens provides guidelines for getting through this adolescent stage successfully and without regrets.

As you navigate through this book's chapters, promise to stay committed to applying at least each coping skill each week. Write down things you hope to achieve through every coping skill. Share your goals with a family member or friend, and stay accountable to them. This will strengthen your commitment to your growth process.

Section 1: Understanding Emotions: The Why, What, and How

Emotions are reactions to situations or circumstances. The type of emotion an individual will feel depends on the circumstance and situation that triggers the emotion. For instance, a person may experience joy when receiving good news or fear when they are in danger. Emotions have a big impact on how individuals live daily. People make several decisions based on their emotions: anger, joy, frustration, sadness, boredom, etc. People also choose hobbies and interests based on the kind of emotions they evoke. Therefore, emotions, while challenging, are not a bad thing; in fact, they are essential to helping you better understand yourself. The goal is to learn how to control, manage, and channel them appropriately, starting by paying attention to them. When you take the time to evaluate your emotions, your life becomes more stable and easier to navigate.

Why Are Emotions Essential?

Emotions drive us to make decisions. [33]

Emotions are a necessary component of human existence because they inform you of your needs and allow you to express them to others and receive assistance. For instance, when you feel depressed and need help, people who are aware can quickly assist you. Emotions not only inform us of how we feel, but they are also what drives us to make decisions for ourselves and the people around us.

Emotions Motivate You

Emotions motivate you to act right in all kinds of situations you encounter. For example, before writing a difficult exam, it's normal to feel anxious about how you will do and how the exam will affect your final grade. Due to this anxiety, you may become motivated to study hard to avoid failing. In this instance, your emotion has become a push towards doing better.

Additionally, being motivated by emotions makes you act in certain ways to increase positive emotions and decrease the possibility of having negative ones. For instance, to avoid circumstances that cause boredom, anxiety, and sadness, you may look for hobbies or social activities that make you feel content, energetic, and happy.

Emotions Help You Understand Others

The emotional expressions of those around you reveal information, just as your emotions reveal vital information to others. Therefore, identifying and responding to other people's emotions aids interpersonal relationships and daily social interaction. It lets you communicate and create stronger, meaningful bonds with family and friends. Furthermore, it allows you to interact with people in different social contexts, such as managing a rude classmate or a dissatisfied customer.

Emotions Influence Your Decisions

Your emotions play a big role in your decision-making, from what you eat for breakfast to your candidate for student council elections. Hence, emotional intelligence is required to possess good decision-making skills.

Emotions Help Others Understand You Better

When interacting with other people, your emotional state leaves clues that people pick up so they can better understand how you feel. These cues could be expressed through body language, such as facial expressions corresponding to your emotions or even how your emotions affect your tone of voice and how you conduct yourself – this may involve verbally stating how you are feeling outright. When you share your feelings with family members or friends, whether it makes them happy, excited, frightened, or sad, you give them insight into the appropriate action they can take when dealing with you.

Psychological and Biological Reason Behind Emotions

The limbic system is a part of the brain that significantly influences emotion. A component of the limbic system, known as the *amygdala*, controls emotion – specifically emotions related to survival, such as fear. According to research, sensory information moves along two pathways in the brain. This information, triggered by emotional experience, first goes to the thalamus and then moves simultaneously to the brain's cortex and the amygdala. The amygdala analyzes the information and quickly sends impulses to the hypothalamus, which activates the autonomic nervous system. On the other hand, the cortex moves through the information more slowly, making humans analyze, assess, and respond to the situation.

Emotions are interrelated with physical reactions, thoughts, and behavior.

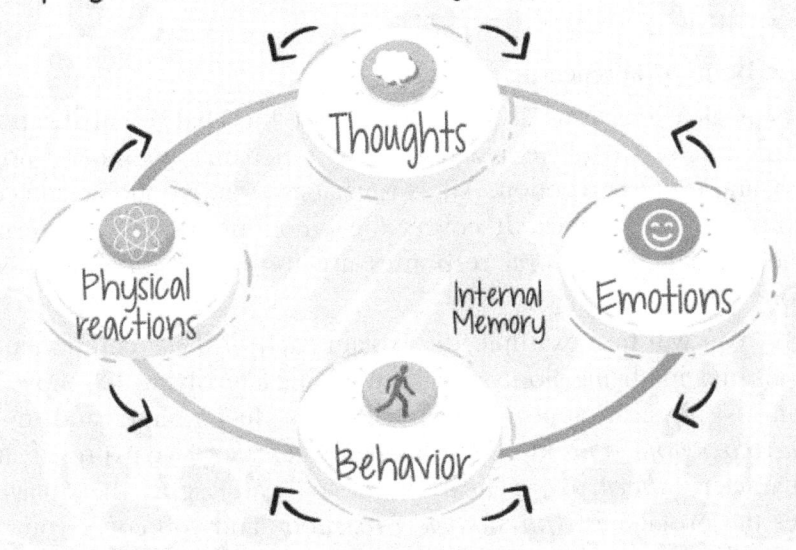

Thoughts — Physical reactions — Internal Memory — Emotions — Behavior

Physiological responses are the automatic reactions people make in situations. These responses could be perspirations, an increased heart rate, etc. They are the responses of the autonomic nervous system to the emotions people feel. The autonomic nervous system manages involuntary bodily reactions and regulates fight-or-flight mode. Many psychologists believe emotions have helped human evolution and survival throughout history because they evoke these physiological reactions.

Interestingly, according to research, the strongest autonomic physiological responses occur when a person's facial expressions closely reflect the presentation of the emotion they are experiencing. Facial expressions are great cues in determining how one physically reacts to an emotion.

How Emotions Are Experienced

Emotion is a subjective mental and conscious response to a specific experience that usually comes with changes in a person's physiology and behavior. Emotional encounters give rise to feelings. Thus, when people don't eat, they feel hunger or pain due to consciousness.

Emotions are divided into four different components:
- Physiological reactions
- Cognitive reactions
- Affect
- Behavioral reactions

Physiological reactions are responsible for the changes in the body's hormone levels. Cognitive reactions are a person's memory, thought process, and event perception. Affect is what gives an emotion a subjective and conscious experience. It covers the emotion's positive or negative condition. Lastly, behavioral responses are the active expression of an emotion.

Here, you will find examples to explain each of these components of emotion. Imagine being alone at night, watching a terrifying TV show. The antagonist's physical appearance makes you feel scared and uneasy (*cognitive reaction*). This kind of thinking makes your face express fear for the character (*affect*). Your heart starts to beat fast as the antagonist pursues the protagonist (*physiological reaction*), and you cover your eyes using your hands out of terror (*a behavioral reaction*).

Increasing Emotional Awareness

Emotional awareness helps in understanding and accepting oneself. Here are three steps to take to increase your emotional awareness.

Pay Attention to Your Feelings

Make it a practice to pay attention to your feelings in various situations throughout the day. If you plan to meet a friend, you will likely observe feelings of excitement; conversely, you might show signs of anxiety before a test. Take note of every emotion you experience and name it in your mind or write it down in a journal. This practice will enable you to keep track of things that make you feel negative emotions and narrow down the activities that provide positive emotions. For instance, drawing or listening to music can help you feel better when stressed.

Rate the Intensity of the Emotion

Once you have recognized and named an emotion, go a step further by rating how severe the impact of the emotion is by marking it on a scale from 1 to 10, with 1 being the mildest and 10 being the strongest. For example, recognize if the anxiety you feel from taking a test is the same as when you come in contact with an animal you fear.

Share How You Feel

Sharing how you feel with others will help you verbalize your emotions. [34]

Sharing your emotions with those you feel safe with will help you practice verbalizing your emotions. Verbalizing emotions makes you feel more connected to friends, partners, and parents, preventing a buildup that induces stress. Make it a habit to express your emotions to a friend or family member. Start with less intense feelings you frequently experience if you feel overwhelmed by sharing too much, and then you can get more personal when you're comfortable.

> Emily, a teenager, struggled with meeting enormous expectations in a quiet suburb. Her family, teacher, and society pressured her to perform well in her academics and extracurricular activities. Emily's stress level increased as she tried to do her numerous responsibilities until it reached a breaking point during a piano lesson. This made Emily open up to her mother about her emotions. When Emily talked to her mother more, she learned about her mother's past troubles. With the help of her family, she reconsidered her priorities, expressed her emotions more, and learned how to manage her life. After this experience, Emily learned the importance of setting limits, asking for help, and putting her well-being above overachievement.

Common Emotions Experienced by Teens

Adolescents frequently experience various emotions at a time. The changes in hormones in their bodies are often responsible for minor alterations in their feelings and emotions. You can be all calm and laid-back one second, then lose your cool the next due to mood swings.

As a teenager, you become vulnerable to these emotions through puberty. You may become too emotional, impatient, and easily excited. Spending hours sobbing over seemingly little issues and becoming overly optimistic about something adults might find bothersome is normal.

Teenagers experience a range of powerful emotions, including anger. It could occasionally cause rebellion, giving your parents the impression that you despise them. It might be stressful and perplexing to experience several different emotions quickly, leading to resentment, anger, aggression, and, in rare instances, violence.

Emotion Journaling Activity

By recording your feelings throughout the day, you can learn to recognize your emotions. You can manually record your activities, mood, and accompanying physical sensations at each point in time by using a reminder that buzzes on your phone every few hours.

Take time to journal how you feel during and after experiencing these emotions:

- Anger _____
- Happiness _____
- Shame _____
- Guilt _____
- Satisfaction _____
- Envy _____
- Annoyance _____
- Sadness _____
- Love _____
- Disappointment _____
- Embarrassment _____
- Fear _____
- Disgust _____
- Surprise _____
- Boredom _____
- Pride _____
- Loneliness _____
- Frustration _____
- Jealousy _____

As you know, emotions serve a wide range of purposes. Emotions can be brief, strong, enduring, transformative, and even complicated. They can influence your behavior and provide the resources and tools to engage in meaningful social interaction.

This section focused on what emotions are and why they are vital and broke down the biological and psychological factors behind emotions. You were also provided insight into how you experience emotions and how to be aware of them. With this information, it becomes clear that both negative and positive emotions are normal and necessary. The goal is not to prevent certain emotions but to manage them. Do not fight what you feel; instead, pay attention to what your emotions convey.

Thank you for taking the time to understand this section and invest in your emotional well-being!

Section 2: The Ups and Downs of Teenage Years

The transitional stage between childhood and adulthood, known as adolescence, is a crucial time in a person's growth and development, emotionally, behaviorally, and physically. Adolescence is even more challenging because changing one area affects other aspects of life. Therefore, your response to these changes can make your adolescent stage satisfying, unique, overwhelming, or confusing.

The body's physical growth and rising hormone levels are responsible for some of the main changes in adolescence. Physical growth alters the hormones, affecting teens' emotional development. As a result, it is normal for teens to show irregular behaviors, self-consciousness, restlessness, and moodiness.

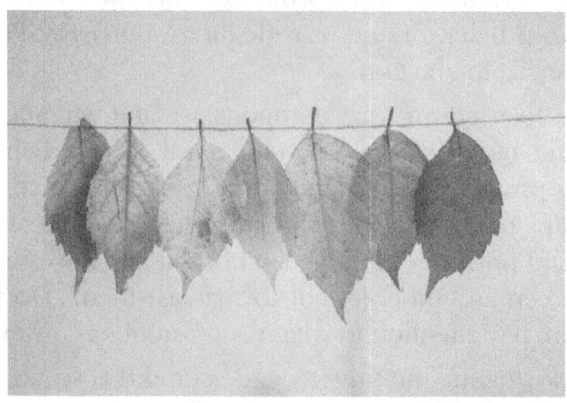

Change is a normal part of adolescence. [35]

As you grow into adolescence, your social world enlarges, which can cause personal and recreational challenges in your life. Difficulties at this stage are normal and will conjure up a need to discover your identity and a desire for freedom.

How These Changes Affect Your Everyday Life

The changes brought on by adolescence will affect your decision-making, mood, and relationships with people. You will sometimes experience intense feelings that make your mood unpredictable. These emotional fluctuations occur partially because your brain is still developing the ability to express and control emotions maturely. In making decisions, you may go through a phase of acting on impulse. Acting on impulse happens because you are still in the process of learning how to make decisions. However, all actions have repercussions, and you need to be aware of the dangers that can accompany them.

Another significant change is your desire to spend time with peers rather than with the family. Detachment from family has to do with your need for independence as you mature. Your family routines, connections, and friendships will change as you become more independent. At this stage, you've started thinking more abstractly, which makes you question various viewpoints. You will constantly find that you unintentionally hurt people because you are unaware of how your actions and words influence others.

Additionally, the change in your appearance will impact your self-esteem. You will become more conscious about your appearance and might become accustomed to comparing your body to others.

10 Problems Teenagers May Face in Today's World

1. They may experience difficulty and stress when managing and prioritizing their time.
2. They engage in unsafe sexual conduct and activity.
3. They desire to be a part of welcoming and encouraging communities outside of their family.
4. They become vulnerable to mental and physical issues.
5. They often face pressure from parents, peers, and society to meet certain expectations.
6. They lack inspiring role models, mentors, and heroes.
7. They have urges to start using drugs and alcohol in unhealthy ways.
8. They are being subjected to toxic and violent information on television and social media.
9. They often experience bullying online and offline.
10. They experience negative body image, which is an unrealistic way of how people see their bodies.

Advice for Going through Challenges in Adolescence

To enjoy a crisis-free adolescence and become a responsible adult, you must learn to make decisions, be assertive, and set and prioritize goals. You also have to learn to take charge of your life, and you can achieve this by adhering to the following:

Know Your Morals

Morals are the things you value and believe in, things you consider good or bad, and things that are most significant to you. You need to have a clear understanding of what your principles are so they can guide you in defining yourself throughout your adolescence.

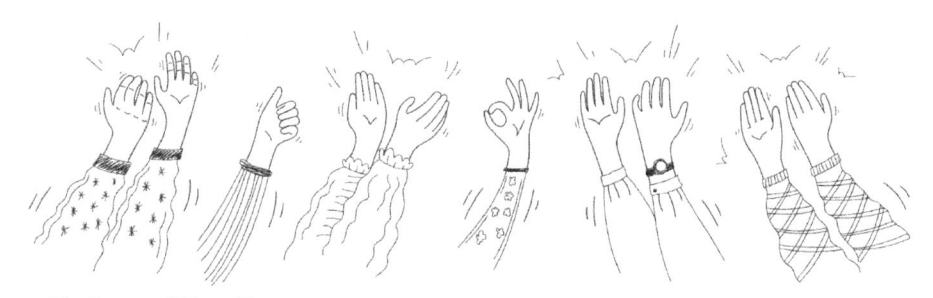

Embrace The Chance

The best period to learn anything is during adolescence. A teenager's developing brain is just as plastic as a child's in its earliest three years. Basic survival skills, including motor skills, vision, and bonding, are prioritized by a child's developing brain. The prefrontal cortex, which is located behind our foreheads, is the portion of the teenage brain that is most pliable. We require our prefrontal cortex, whether we're studying a language, a sport, a musical instrument, a science, an art form, or non-cognitive abilities like self-control, empathy, and social skills. There has never been such an opportunity to learn and apply these abilities. Therefore, embrace the chance to develop skills during this period because, after adolescence, the plasticity of our brains substantially decreases.

Form Healthy Habits

Form healthy sleeping, eating, and exercise habits to enhance your growth.

The brain requires a lot of energy for it to work. Our brain uses 20% of the foods we consume as energy. It is not too late to improve if you have already developed bad eating habits. Start small and find areas where you may improve, such as drinking more water, eating fewer processed foods, eating more fruits and vegetables, and avoiding added sugar and saturated fats.

Plan to go moving and be active every day! According to studies, exercise helps reduce anxiety and sadness, lowers disease risk, improves focus and self-confidence, and calms anger. Plan out your week to make sure exercising is one of your top priorities, whether you can set a reasonable target, like 10,000 steps per day, or find an activity you enjoy.

Sleep is also important for the development of the body and mind. Although it seems simple, teenagers' body clocks naturally keep them awake later at night and urges them to sleep more in the morning. To lower anxiety levels, clear toxins that accumulate in the brain, and reduce dangerous or emotional decisions, make sure you get 8-10 hours of sleep *every night.* Create a pleasant and relaxing sleeping environment, work from your desk rather than from your bed, and avoid using electronics and sugary meals right before bedtime.

Discover Your Interests, Explore New Opportunities

Discovering your passion is frequently connected to fulfillment and happiness on an individual level. For this reason, if you want your adolescence to be fulfilling, you must discover your interests. It takes trying out several activities to find and explore your interests. It is uncommon to be passionate about something we have little knowledge of. To fall in love with a goal or work on it daily, you must first have some understanding of it and become familiar with its difficulties and challenges. Remember that discovering your interests is a process that takes time and doesn't happen all at once. Your interests might change over the years. *That's alright.*

It's a good feeling to believe you have a skill. There are various skills you can learn, such as computer skills, teaching, writing, drawing, and acting. These skills could help you earn money and increase your level of independence. You must, however, be prepared to deal with and get through disappointments. You must be willing to put in as much time and effort as is necessary.

Communicate With Family and Friends

Usually, when things are hard, we turn to our friends and family. To have constant support whenever we need it, we have to be able to communicate openly with these people. Communication with family and friends about good and terrible experiences is extremely useful for your mental health. On the other hand, isolation may be harmful.

Generally speaking, our family and friends are the ones who know us the best and are, therefore, in the best position to offer counsel. They are aware of our identities and past experiences. This implies that they can offer advice based on circumstances specific to our personalities and ideals.

Take Pride in Yourself

Many successful people got to their positions today because of their confidence. A positive view of yourself will enable you to reach your goals quickly. Believe you can overcome difficult situations and succeed. Do not let people's criticism deter you from making an effort. Making decisions, good and bad, is what maturing is all about.

Here is a personal story that shows the essence of this developmental period. The journey of this particular adolescent experience shows that all teenagers go through similar situations, and you are not alone.

"I was thrilled that the time had come for me to enter adolescence when I was thirteen. I would have more freedom and responsibility. I would improve my writing skills and abilities. Being a teenager was a thrilling experience for me. I was so focused on the delights of adolescence that I nearly ignored my sister's advice. I did not understand it at first but later realized what she meant. Life as a teenager has as much sweetness as it does sour, I (and many others) realized.

Being a teen, I liked the sweets adolescence brings. Your parents give you more freedom; you can have some privacy. Your skills begin to develop and become sharper. My writing changed, becoming more in-depth and descriptive. You can also get employed and make your own money. Of course, you need your parents' permission first."

As stated, being a teenager is not always cheerful and fun; sometimes, it may feel like you're living in a nightmare! Adults have high expectations of you as you get older. Backstabbing and peer pressure start to take place. You begin to make new friends and lose old ones. You get additional schoolwork, which only makes the situation worse.

15 LIFE SKILLS FOR TEENAGERS

- [ ] Money Management
- [ ] Time Management
- [ ] Respectfulness
- [ ] Communication
- [ ] Organizational Skills
- [ ] Career Exploration
- [ ] Educational Planning
- [ ] Emergency
- [ ] Navigate Technology
- [ ] Self-Advocacy
- [ ] Coping
- [ ] Decision-Making
- [ ] Self-Care
- [ ] Interpersonal Skills
- [ ] Emotional Skills
- [ ] Health and Nutrition
- [ ] Home Maintenance
- [ ] Personal Hygiene

Teen life may be very stressful. A teenager can hardly breathe with all that's going on. From my experience, adolescence can be a drag with absolutely no fun at some point, then, at another, it offers so much fun. That's how life goes!

Although adolescence is a time of incredible growth and change, it can also be challenging. During this stage, teenagers sometimes struggle with issues like knowing who they are and what they want. Do not hesitate to ask for assistance to get through tough times. There are a lot of resources, both in person and online, so don't be afraid to ask for help if you start struggling more than usual.

Section 3: Mindfulness – Your Emotional Landscape

The teenage years are filled with many opportunities and risks. It is also when you get a significant amount of stress triggers as you go through your daily demands from school, body changes, parents, and keeping up with peers. You're likely to get more negative pressure at this age due to exposure to certain experiences like trauma, violence, racism, homophobia, and, on some occasions, abuse. It isn't just about these pressures but the fact that everyone expects you to have a healthy sense of yourself and be able to regulate your emotions no matter how hard they are to decipher. This is a critical season of your growth into adulthood, so you need to practice mindfulness to grow with healthy emotions – and here's how you can do that.

Mindfulness helps you become more aware of your surroundings.[36]

What Is Mindfulness?

Mindfulness isn't an extraordinary skill that needs special training. It's a daily part of your life. It's your ability to live in the present moment, becoming aware of where you are and what you're doing. When you're mindful, you become careful of your reactions to things around you. You're also not overwhelmed with the happenings around you, and you learn to be more attentive on purpose, approaching things and people in a non-judgmental way.

Mindfulness is your *emotional landscape*. It is a time when you're actively aware of your surroundings and inner state – again, in a *non-judgmental way*. It allows you to pay attention to the present moment with curiosity, openness, kindness, and the ability to blend. According to neuroscience research, practicing mindfulness improves your immune system and increases your empathy and ability to retain memory. The practice affects your mental and physical well-being. In this section, you'll learn practical ways to apply mindfulness and observe and acknowledge your emotions without judgment.

3 Significances Of Mindfulness

To have control of your emotions is to be fully conscious of them. When you practice mindfulness, you do not allow your stress and emotions to decide how you react to people or situations. Here's how mindfulness can create a mental space to manage your triggers:

Be Aware of Your Emotions

When you're mindful, you tend to pay attention to the present without judgment. You're well aware of when your emotions surge to the surface, and rather than reacting out of impulse, you stop to recognize and process them. Emotions, even the ones you don't like, should not be met with shame or disapproval. You are human, and feeling all emotions - even the ugly ones - is okay. This type of awareness makes room for mental space between your triggers and reactions; thus, you learn that you control your responses to situations regardless of what drives you emotionally.

Learning to Recognize Your Triggers

With mindfulness, you can easily identify your emotional triggers instead of being overwhelmed and controlled by them. You can step back and try to observe what caused those emotional reactions - there's always a cause for any reaction, and when you carefully observe the cause, you'll find the triggers. This helps you understand the root of your emotions and allows you to address them more accurately.

Learning to Pause

You can develop and grow your ability to create pauses before any and every reaction. Remember that emotions can be extreme, whether they are positive or negative, and you don't want to go overboard. The paused moment allows you to take a deep breath, look into the situation, and choose a better and more responsible response rather than acting out of impulse or unintentionally.

Practical Mindful Exercises for You

Your emotions have needs, and applying a mindful exercise helps you address them accordingly. All exercises have either mental or physical benefits. Here are some mindful exercises you can put into practice:

Deep Breathing

Instructions for deep breathing

Step 1: Place your hands on your lower belly and focus on breathing into that area.

Step 2: Place your hands on either side of your rib cage and expand them outward with your breath.

Step 3: Place your hands on your chest (just below your collarbones) and fill that area with your breath.

Step 4: Hold your breath for a few seconds, then exhale from the upper chest, followed by the ribcage, and finally, the belly.

In this exercise, you intentionally control your breath while mindfully focusing on it. You use the diaphragm to make slow breaths, and your body feels relaxed in the process.

Body Scanning

How to Do a Body Scan Meditation

- Get comfortable
- Close your eyes & focus on your breath
- Bring awareness to a specific part of your body
- Spend 20-60 seconds noticing sensations
- Imagine tension decreasing with each breath
- Release your focus on that part of your body
- Move to the next part of your body and continue
- If your thoughts wander, gently bring your awareness back
- After several scans, let your awareness travel across your whole body
- Release your focus & come back to your surroundings

This is where you bring your focus to various parts of your body. You spend 10 to 30 seconds on each of them, for example, your toes, fingers, stomach, and feet. When you bring your complete attention to a specific body part, you'll feel warmth, tingling, pain, or pressure.

Mind Journaling

Mind journaling can help you clear your head. [37]

Here, you get to ease your mind off the many noises that consume it. Give your full attention and sit in silence until the noise fades away. Have your journal beside you to jot down whatever comes to mind without leaving anything out. Whatever prompt you get can help guide your writing.

Mindful Walking

Mindful walking can help you become more focused on yourself. [38]

Find a quiet spot where you will not easily be distracted, start walking at your natural pace, and keep your attention on your feet as they touch the ground. Become aware of each step you take, how your body moves, and how your weight suddenly becomes balanced. If your mind begins to wander, gently bring it back to your walking.

Five Senses Exercise

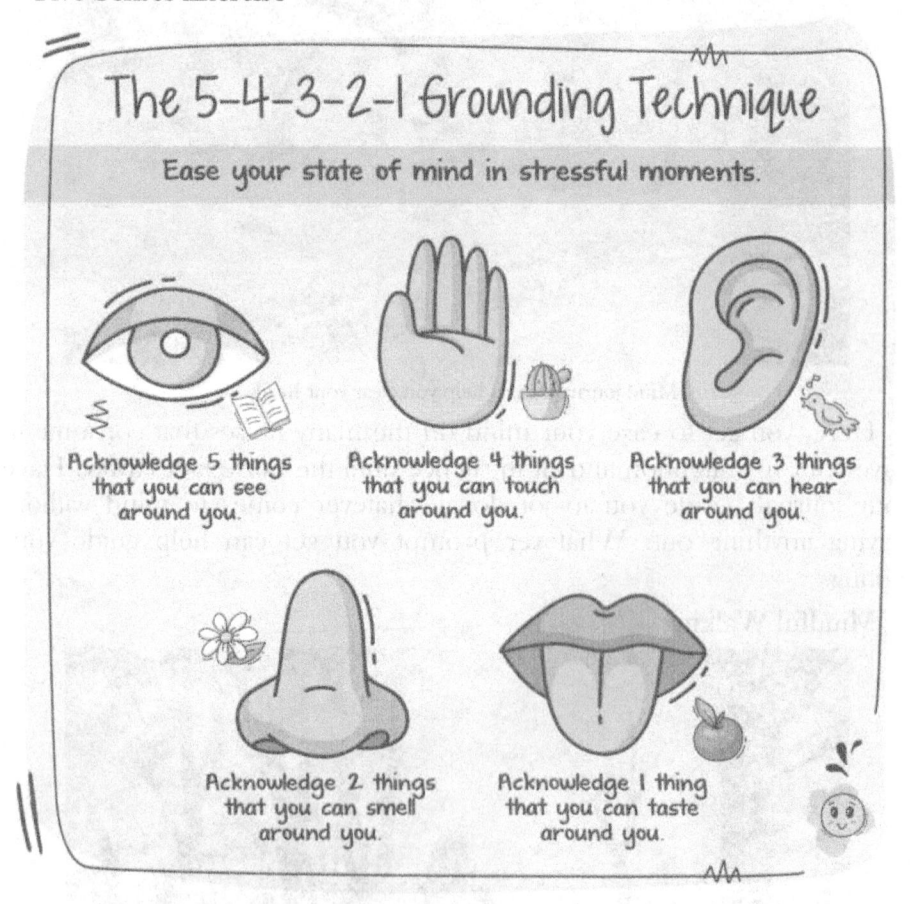

The 5-4-3-2-1 Grounding Technique

Ease your state of mind in stressful moments.

Acknowledge 5 things that you can see around you.

Acknowledge 4 things that you can touch around you.

Acknowledge 3 things that you can hear around you.

Acknowledge 2 things that you can smell around you.

Acknowledge 1 thing that you can taste around you.

Pause and focus on your surroundings. Identify the first five things you see, four things you can touch, three you can hear, two you can smell, and one you can taste. Try to engage each of your senses on those things one at a time and experience those moments through your senses.

Observing Your Emotions Without Judgment

It's best to see your emotions as they are and learn to accept them rather than try to suppress them. Feel the flow they bring, and cultivate ways to navigate them. You can imagine them as a large, ever-changing landscape; sometimes, they are pleasant, and other times not so pleasant. When you come to accept them, you promote mindfulness. Here's how you can embrace them:

Emotions are non-judgmental awareness. To practice a healthy form of mindfulness, you need empathy. Before you can empathize with others, you need empathy for yourself. Have compassion when these emotions arise, acknowledge them as a natural part of your being, and allow yourself room for self-acceptance.

Imagine emotions as passing clouds. As mentioned earlier, your emotions are like a landscape with weather. Sometimes it rains, other times it's sunny. Your role is to embrace the weather and control your reaction to it. Let the weather happen – let your emotions occur and pass, just like the daily weather. Don't cling to them.

Your emotions are a part of you; accept them for what they are, and don't let them get the best of you. When they emerge, be observant and practice the above mindfulness tips. Journal your thoughts, write down your observations of your triggers and how to best avoid them. Don't give in to the pressures around you. Be your own boss and develop your mental strength; it matters a lot in becoming a strong adult.

Section 4: The Power of Positive Thinking

The power positive thinking has on human life is amazing, and the reality that your world can change for the better just by a change in your thought patterns is something you should take advantage of. This section will address positive thinking and its psychological and physical benefits. Furthermore, you will learn practical strategies for cultivating positive thinking and some exercises you can practice to help you cultivate this power. So, what is positive thinking, and does it connote an avoidance of problems? Find out here!

The Purpose of Positive Thinking

Positive thinking is not about repressing negative emotions, which is a big misrepresentation of the term. Bad days, grief, anger, sorrow, loss, and fear are all part of life. No one can guarantee happy days – just happy perspectives. As with positive emotions, negative emotions are just one end of the spectrum. Both negative and positive emotions are vital for living; repressing and avoiding negative emotions only makes things overwhelming and hurtful.

Positive thinking helps you see the good in every situation. [39]

Positive thinking is not a "cure it all" drug; neither is it about faking it or pretending. So, what is positive thinking? Positive thinking is seeing "the good" in every situation. It deals with every unpleasant issue productively and positively. It involves techniques like replacing negative thoughts with positive ones, stopping pessimistic thoughts in their tracks using distractions and relaxation methods, and managing problems by breaking them down into smaller chunks that can be handled.

Psychological and Physical Benefits of Positive Thinking

There are many benefits associated with positive thinking. It enables you to accomplish most things you want to do despite the heavy challenges involved. Positive thinking helps you overcome stress by conditioning your mind to focus on things that matter. Follows are more benefits of positive thinking.

Positive Attitude

Positive-thinking individuals have a positive attitude toward life and surround themselves with happy people who ooze positive energy. They go beyond immediate situations and challenges to see and affirm the positive. People with a positive outlook focus more on productive reactions than what they cannot control. You can see this in how they handle work, struggles, and the people around them. It is not about always being happy but about prioritizing healthy habits that improve the present and near future rather than dwelling on past difficulties.

Stress Relief

Positive thinking relieves you of the stress that comes with negative emotions, like worrying and anxiousness. A positive mindset can effectively handle stressful situations, and people who adopt this mindset are likely to devise plans and seek counsel if needed instead of wallowing in self-pity and defeat because it enables them to develop good stress-coping skills in challenging times.

Enhances Immunity

The mind is proven to be a powerful entity that can positively or negatively affect the body. A major area where your attitudes and thoughts can do the most damage or good is your immunity. A trigger in your brain that comes from negative emotions can result in a frailer immune system response, causing the flu. For example, a person anticipating a school performance may dread their performance and beat themselves up about it once they're done, or they can find the joy of performing and be proud of their accomplishments and the fact that they put themselves out there. The latter tend to demonstrate a more powerful immune response than individuals with a pessimistic perception of their performance.

Boosts Wellness

Other than positive thinking influencing your immunity and ability to manage stress, it also influences your health in general, from reducing depression and risk of death associated with cardiovascular disease to decreasing the risk of death from cancer, respiratory conditions, and infections. A positive mindset is proven to help in prolonging life span.

More Enhanced Resilience

Resilience is about perseverance – resilient people show heart and grit in the presence of trauma. Instead of the crises getting the better of them, they surmount them.

You might be surprised that the art of thinking positively plays a role in building resilience in an individual. People with a positive attitude always consider what they can do when faced with a challenge. Giving up is never an option with them. You can enjoy long-term and short-term benefits when you foster positive thinking in challenging situations.

Practical Strategies for Cultivating Positive Thinking

Here are some strategies to guide you into becoming a positive thinker:

- Devour books and articles about positive attitudes and how to be optimistic and reflect on your reading.
- Do not associate with negative-minded people who see negativity in everything.
- Associate with optimistic and happy people.
- Find motivation through the actions of individuals with the desire and passion to improve in their respective fields.
- Employ the services of your imagination to see only positive outcomes no matter how messed up the situation might be. With this, you will only attract positive outcomes.
- Talk to yourself using affirmations and positive words like "I can."
- Life will always throw curve balls your way; look for a reason to smile often. This process will cause you to feel good inwardly and maintain a cheerful disposition when relating to others.

Exercises for Positive-Thinking

Below are some of the exercises you can practice to help you harness the power of positive thinking.

Gratitude Journaling

Gratitude journaling can help you see life in a more positive light. [40]

Practicing gratitude and writing down what you are grateful for has many benefits. It makes you see life differently. As often as you express grateful thoughts, you will feel positive about life. Gratitude journaling will enhance your health and positive emotions and give you many reasons not to give up in the face of challenges.

Positive Affirmations

When you affirm good things about yourself, you will maintain these good traits. You can do this by changing your perspective from "I am afraid" to "I am bold" or, instead of affirming "I am terrible at math," you can tell yourself, "I may not be happy about my test score, but I won't give up! I'll take more time to improve to do better on future tests." Positive affirmations like these help you eliminate negative emotions by focusing on thoughts that increase your productivity rather than discourage you. Eventually, your self-talk will evolve to where you always speak about yourself with respect and positivity.

Visualization

Vision Board

DREAMS

I WANT TO TRY

INSPIRATION

GOALS

PLACES I WILL GO

Seeing yourself as successful will help you accomplish great things, now and in the future. Close your eyes and imagine the feelings, smells, and sights you will encounter when you accomplish your dream. You can take it a step further by drawing the things you have imagined and placing these pictures in an area where you will see them every morning to remind you of your pursuit.

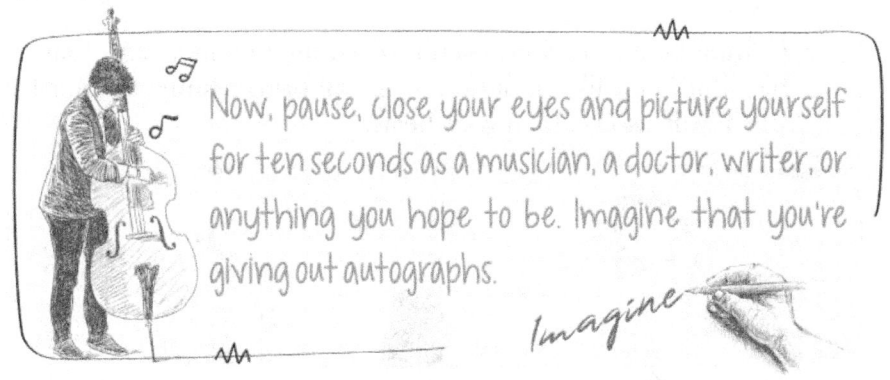

> Now, pause, close your eyes and picture yourself for ten seconds as a musician, a doctor, writer, or anything you hope to be. Imagine that you're giving out autographs.
>
> *Imagine*

Random Acts of Kindness

Offering a helping hand to others is a great way to boost your mental health. Being good to others is doing good to yourself. It will enhance both your physical and emotional well-being and reduce stress. Always be on the lookout to show somebody kindness; even if it is the only thing you accomplish that day, *it is worth it.*

More random acts of kindness you can do in school, at home, or outside:

- Creating colorful and thoughtful thank you cards to show appreciation to healthcare workers.

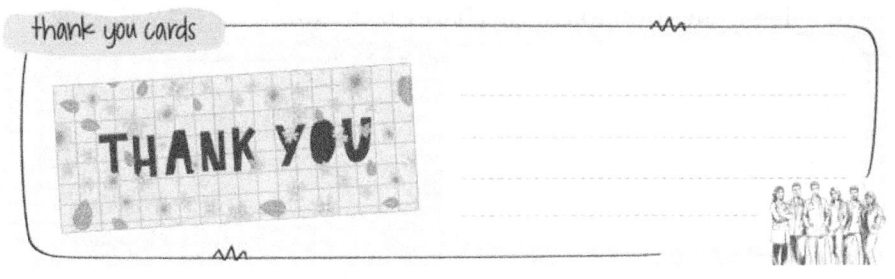

> thank you cards
>
> THANK YOU

- Going on a trash patrol in your neighborhood with a friend. Collecting and recycling litter are a few ways to be nice to the planet!

- Compliment a teacher, friend, or family member daily. Say one nice thing you like about them. It will bring a smile to their face, which will also gladden your heart.

- Offer to tutor a fellow student struggling with a particular subject you're really great at!

- Declutter your closet and donate the things you no longer use or have outgrown to a local charity near you.

- Write a thank you note to your parents or grandparents for the gift they got you and for supporting you all through the year.

Physical Activities

Physical activities like taking a hip hop class, walking your dog, or playing sports with your pairs can boost your confidence and make you smile more. They minimize stress, stimulate the release of *endorphins* (feel-good hormones), and cause you to be more innovative. Go on a fun date with your friends and watch heart-warming movies, funny TV shows, and family-friendly stand-up comedians that will cause you to giggle and laugh your heart out. It will relieve stress and improve your overall health.

Practicing positive thinking is essential to your physical and emotional well-being. Its impact cannot be overstated as it aids in forming your actions, outlook on life, and attitudes. A positive mindset set, when properly cultivated, exposes you to endless possibilities. We hope the strategies and exercises in this section lead you to develop a happier outlook on life and attract more positivity.

Section 5: Techniques for Stress Management

Teenagers get stressed when pressured because they are just beginning to understand certain emotions. Stress is not all bad; it's just another emotional reaction. Too much of it, however, can harm your health. Stress is your response to external pressure, such as submission deadlines or making difficult decisions. In this section, you'll learn the techniques to manage your stress properly and how stress affects your mental and physical health.

Stress Is a Common Experience

Stress is a universal experience. [41]

Do you sometimes wish certain negative and unusual emotions didn't exist? You might wish they weren't part of you because they make you uncomfortable. It's okay to feel that way – it's natural. We all face stress, although some people's triggers may be more difficult to manage than others. Your triggers could stem from peer interactions, school responsibilities, or family dynamics. When you're aware of your triggers, you can better prepare for them. When you cannot cope with your stress, it harms you in the long run. Here are ways stress affects your mental and physical health:

Effects on Mental Health

Your teenage years influence your social and emotional development and shape your mental well-being. There are many ways stress can affect your mental health; some of them include the following:

- **Worry and anxiety:** When your stress is prolonged or not properly dealt with, it can cross into worry and anxiety for future outcomes. It is healthy to feel worried or mild anxiety occasionally, but prolonged stress keeps your mind preoccupied with unnecessary events and harms your mental health.

- **It leads to depression:** When you cannot curb your stress, it builds up and accumulates over time. Then, you start to experience stages of loneliness and sadness and will likely lose interest in things that once excited you.

- **You have difficulties concentrating:** Your mind tunes out of the present moment when you fail to cope with stress. This makes it difficult to focus on a task, leading to frustrations and struggles in your academics.

Effects on Physical Health

In the sections above, you learned that the mind controls how the body feels and reacts. The mind is the center of a person. If you cannot handle your stress, it will not only negatively affect your mental health, but it will gradually begin to seep into your physical body, leading to physical illnesses. Here are ways stress affects you physically:

- **A weak immune system:** Your state of mind reflects on your immune system. If your mind is unhealthy, it will impact your immune system. You'll be more susceptible to illness with low immunity. Stress on your body looks like exhaustion and lethargy – often misconstrued as laziness.

- **You can experience changes in appetite.** When you become stressed, there are changes your body makes. For example, you begin to eat excessively or have little to no appetite.

Everyone has a distinct immune system and responds to stress differently. Some of these effects are less severe in some individuals and more severe in others. Without the right coping mechanisms, stress becomes overwhelming and, in dire cases, *chronic*.

Stress Reduction Techniques

Here are some helpful techniques to better manage stress:

Breathing Techniques

Steady breathing directly impacts our nervous system, calming you down in stressful environments and clearing your head. To practice this activity, inhale deeply and count to three. For count 1, breathe in deeply, hold for count 2, and breathe out for count 3. This relaxes your body, reducing stress simultaneously.

Physical Activity

Exercise can help you relieve stress.[42]

Exercise is another way to get out of your stressful mind and into your body. You can consider small exercises to fit in regularly, like walking, jogging, dancing, or playing any physical sports requiring you to move your body. When you do this, your body releases a chemical called *endorphins* that acts as a natural stress reliever. Find a physical activity that appeals to your interests; there are plenty of options out there, from Yoga and Zumba to tennis and football. Yoga is worth getting into because it involves physical and mental exercise, teaching you how to clear your mind and practice steady breathing.

Time Management and Organization

To have a stress-free day, plan ahead. A routine can counter the stress that comes with a lack of stability and security. If you don't have it all figured out and are unsure about the next task you should be doing, the pressure can set you back. Overcome this by creating a to-do list. Prioritize your tasks in order of importance and set a reasonable time frame to complete them.

Taking Up Hobbies

Are you a music lover? Do you love art and crafts? There's no better way to handle stress than to channel them into a positive outlet. Working out your skills will soothe your mood, relieving your stress. A good example of using art as a form of practicing mindfulness is through scribbling. Scribbling is relaxing and addresses your stress and anxiety immediately. It helps you focus on processes and not outcomes by embracing your limitations and putting your expectations aside.

In the box below, write or draw out everything that seems to stress or put you under pressure. All you need is paper, pencils, or crayons for this exercise. Take all you've written and tear it up (or squash it into a tiny ball), reducing and letting go of your anxiety.

Being a teenager requires you to process lots of emotions, and sometimes, it can be hard to manage since this is all new to you. There are tested techniques that you can utilize to help manage your stress triggers. In this section, you've learned of the effects of stress and how it affects your mental and physical health. Be patient with the techniques you try. It may take some time for your mind and body to respond, but the good thing is that you're on the right track for change.

Section 6: Bouncing Back from Setbacks

A peek into the life of a popular, successful figure like Oprah Winfrey will help you see setbacks in a different light. She was born into poverty and raised by a single mother. She went through sexual, mental, and physical abuse as a child and ran away from home when she was just thirteen. At fourteen, she became pregnant and lost the child almost immediately after birth. Aside from her setbacks in her childhood, she also suffered setbacks in her career. She was dismissed from her job because she was considered unfit for television. However, she didn't just give in to the failures; she persevered, and today, she is a household name.

Setbacks are situations, challenges, and events that cause you to lose progress in life. At some point in your life, you will face setbacks, whether in the form of rejections or failures. Coming back from setbacks makes your resolve for success better and stronger. Setbacks are one of the requirements for success. It gives you opportunities for growth and change and builds resilience, a vital life skill to overcome challenges and hurdles life throws your way. As long as you're alive, there will be an obstacle to overcome. What you don't hear is how having one can give you purpose and should be considered an opportunity for learning. So, how do you cultivate these vital life skills? And how do they enable you to face obstacles and difficulties with grit and heart? Read on!

Practical Steps for Cultivating Resilience

Setbacks can help you build resilience. [45]

Setbacks happen to all, but one thing remains: setbacks are only a temporary detour. It is an opportunity to return stronger, with a better strategy to push again. Knowing that setbacks are integral to living, there are methods you can use to help you deal with failure, position yourself, and persevere with vigor. Below are the practical steps for cultivating resilience:

Acknowledge Emotions

It is normal to feel sad and discouraged after a setback. *Oddly, it is one way of measuring how close you are to your goal.* Ignoring how you feel or trying to fake that you are okay when you are not would only compound the issue.

There is nothing wrong with missing out on a dream. Ask anyone who has accomplished something great, and you'd be surprised at how many times they hit a snag on the road before their breakthrough. These individuals immediately tackled the elephant in the room and ensured it had been dealt with before forging ahead.

Go through the failure, cry if you must, but allow yourself to *feel*. Brushing it aside won't make it go away. Instead, it can make you give up.

Change your Mindset

At this point, you can either see yourself as a failure and talk down to yourself or dust off the dirt and forge ahead, seeing it as a setup for a major comeback. How do you see yourself? Are your thoughts healthy? Are you stuck on viewing things from one narrow perspective? Do you motivate yourself with your self-talk or discourage your efforts? Which of these options do you think are likely to lead to success?

When you see setbacks as temporary, you realize they are simply there to ensure you are determined on your path and that you - *and you alone* - define your life based on your reactions.

Set New Goals

Strategizing after a temporary detour involves setting smart goals that align with your dream - now with the lessons learned from previous experience.

Seek Support

Seeking support will help you learn different ways to cope with setbacks.."

You are not alone. Countless individuals have walked the road you are on. Sitting down with them and hearing how they overcame their setbacks will teach you not to give up. You might even find they have gone through worse yet are still standing. With their experience, they could guide you on what to do. This support can be found online or in your local community. They could be your friends, church-goers, colleagues at work, etc.

Several Setbacks and How to Overcome Them

Below are some setbacks and ways to overcome them.

Academic Setbacks or Failures: Some ways to overcome failures include the following:

- Figure out what caused the failure.
- Come up with a plan that goes beyond getting back on track and focuses on remaining on track. These plans entail new strategies like changing your study time, finding new friends who can help, etc.
- Contemplate your experience and the previous strategies that led to where you are and figure out how not to repeat it.

Write out some of the challenges you are currently experiencing in your studies and how you plan on overcoming them.

Friendship Issues

- Improve your communication skills with either help from books or online or by talking to your friend about what is missing.
- Take a time-out – give both you and your friend space to breathe and think.
- Be positive. Do not resort to blame or accusations for the setback.
- Set expectations. Be specific as to what you are after. Share your needs with your friends and have them share theirs.
- Socialize with new friends.
- Get support. Discuss the situation with another person for counsel on how to go about it.
- Move on if you have done your best, but the friend stubbornly refuses to forgive and move on.

Do you have a good friend you are no longer on good terms with? What are you doing to mend fences?

Rejection From Extracurricular Activities

Rejection is the building block of life. Here is how to overcome it.

- See rejection as part of life
- Acknowledge what happened
- Allow yourself to go through the emotions
- Remain healthy. You are the most important person in your destiny

- You are not the rejection, so don't let it determine how you should live
- Learn from the experience of rejection

The last time you were rejected from joining your favorite club in school, what steps did you take to overcome such rejection?

Family Issues

- Work as a team in looking for headways
- Listen to each other and see things from the other person's point of view
- Arrange a meeting to meet up and talk things over
- Seek professional help

Your parents are in a major disagreement with your grandparents. What are you doing to get all of them in the same room for a peaceful resolution?

Setbacks are a given and should be expected. They are temporary detours, and overcoming them leads to success. Many individuals shy away from a setback, allowing it to deter their paths. They throw in the towel too easily. Not only do setbacks build resilience, but you won't find a success story without them. View setbacks differently today and watch how amazing your result will be from now on.

Section 7: Creating Healthy Relationships

Healthy relationships play a vital role in equipping one's ability to socialize with people and adapt to the environment around them. Your mode of relating with people differs from person to person. This is because of the distinguishable role these people play in your life.

For instance, how you relate with your family members is quite different from how you would normally relate with your friends, teachers, community members, and even your boyfriend or girlfriend, as the case may be. There's usually a subconscious attribution of a boundary as regards the kind of information you discuss or the activity you perform with them. Your relationship with each person is valid, but creating a healthy relationship with them will require you to clearly define their roles so that boundaries are not overstepped.

Relationships majorly contribute to your mental and emotional well-being. At this stage of your life, recognizing the importance of communication, living respectfully, and setting boundaries in your relationship will improve your quality of life. These factors justify the nature of your relationships, determining whether they are healthy or unhealthy.

The Role of Communication, Mutual Respect, and Boundaries in Your Relationships

One can be in an unhealthy relationship and not be aware of it. Teenagers can get caught up in a people-pleasing mentality that costs them their overall well-being. You must pay attention to the following factors and understand how they make or break your relationships.

Communication

Healthy communication will allow you to feel heard and valued.[45]

Healthy relationships are characterized by honest and open communication. This allows you to express yourself and get insight into the personality of those around you. If your relationships do not allow you to share your experiences and communicate your needs sincerely, they won't last long. Communication makes you feel heard and valued, establishing mutual understanding and trust. Miscommunication, on the other hand, leads to problems and hurt feelings that could've been avoided.

Mutual Respect

Respect deserves to be prioritized in every relationship; without it, it is impossible to have a healthy relationship. Signs of respect are usually seen in the manner of communication, tone, and choice of words.

Relationships are only valued and longed for when there is a show of respect. Being respectful will preserve your honor in a relationship.

Boundaries

No two people in a relationship share the same needs or interests. Situations arise that could cause you to have a divided interest. Your desires may differ as the other's desires may push one of your boundaries. A healthy relationship respects boundaries and avoids taking actions that cause harm. Irrespective of the form of these boundaries, physical or emotional, acknowledging your loved one's needs and limits lays the foundation for a healthy relationship.

Differences between Healthy and Unhealthy Relationships

There are several telltale signs that a relationship is healthy or unhealthy. Use these signs to identify the nature of your present relationships and know what to watch out for.

Acceptance

Being able to accommodate the presence of those around you despite their imperfections differentiates a healthy relationship from an unhealthy one. A healthy relationship cultivates acceptance by focusing on the positive qualities of the other individual rather than dwelling on their flaws.

Honesty

Unlike an unhealthy relationship where there's a lack of communication and both individuals cannot express their feelings and share ideas, a healthy relationship fosters honesty. You can openly share your thoughts and express your feelings, knowing fully well that your partner will give you a listening ear. This kind of transparency prevents the need to keep secrets, which can be damaging.

Show of Support

People involved in healthy relationships always support each other's personal development. They are committed to their goals and motivate each other to be the very best version of themselves by offering a helping hand when necessary. Contrary to this form of relationship, an unhealthy relationship is selfish. No one looks out for the other, and those involved always feel isolated.

Importance of Recognizing Red Flags in Relationships

A red flag in a relationship *is any sign of manipulation or unhealthy behaviors*. Usually, these signs are not obvious when they arise, which is why they have long-term effects. However, these red flags become more problematic and uncontrollable when not addressed in due time. These red flags include abusive communication, aggressiveness, and narcissism (the person seems only concerned with themselves, their story, their troubles, etc.). This could be a relationship with a friend or even a family member. Identifying behavior patterns will help you evaluate who's in your inner circle.

Understanding what issues in a relationship can be resolved and worked on and which require separation will help you determine if you should continue in the relationship or leave it behind. Signs like these are often subtle and present themselves in your relationships when you least expect them. They can cause harm to your mental and physical well-being if not properly addressed. Hence, it is necessary to recognize them immediately when they show up.

Tips for Establishing and Maintaining Healthy Relationships

The following tips will help you establish and maintain a healthy relationship with those around you, especially in this digital age:

- Do not betray the trust of those around you. When people trust you, it shows that they believe in your person. Betraying their trust can change their perception of you and breed hatred. Trust can also be lost when you pry into their online space.

- Learn to respect each other's privacy both online and on sight. Your friend will naturally open up to you concerning issues they know you could help them with. However, in some personal situations, when they do not, avoid forcing the words out of their mouths unless they willingly open up to you. On social media, communicate your expectations on online privacy earlier in the relationship and respect each other's limits.

- Reciprocate kind gestures and sacrifices. Do not always be at the receiving end, believing you deserve every kind gesture. You must also return favors when it is in your capacity to. This will strengthen the bond of your relationship, as it is a show of empathy and care.
- Adopt a supportive attitude in your relationships, especially when the other party is about achieving a new feat. It will be great motivation for them to keep moving forward.
- Avoid distractions during quality time, whether online or on sight. If you are making time for each other online, be as present as possible since you cannot be in the same room. Onsight, turn off phone notifications and concentrate on the person in front of you.

It is good to reflect on your relationship with your peers so that you know when to adjust your behaviors towards them. One way to ensure you maintain healthy bonds is to work through your-and their-emotions using journaling. Monitor behaviors and know the kind of association to look out for. Some ideas for your journaling pages could be a title page, Goals, Daily/Weekly spread, Habit tracker, and Progress chart. These are just a few; feel free to add to your pages.

_____ date: __/__/__

S M T W T F S

5 Minute Journaling

date:

Notes

Daily Reflections

DATE: _____

Today I Felt:
_____
_____
_____
_____
_____

Today I Learned:
_____
_____
_____
_____

Today I am Greatful for:
_____
_____
_____
_____
_____
_____
_____
_____

Reflections:
_____
_____
_____
_____
_____
_____
_____
_____
_____
_____
_____
_____
_____

YEAR: _____

| JANUARY | FEBRUARY | MARCH |

| APRIL | MAY | JUNE |

| JULY | AUGUST | SEPTEMBER |

| OCTOBER | NOVEMBER | DECEMBER |

Section 8: Social Media and Mental Health

The use of social media in today's world is more prominent than ever. A greater percentage of the teenagers you will come across today are either signed up on a social media platform or are looking forward to doing so. Platforms like Facebook, WhatsApp, and Twitter (now called "X"), among others, have made communication easier. They are great for entertainment, but with their many benefits, there are also downsides which can pose as threat to the relationships you have built in the past or about building.

There have been certain cases where individuals lost job opportunities after their social media accounts were screened, whereas some received warm commendations. When properly utilized, social media will do more good than harm to your mental health and your image as a person and a brand.

Social Media - Its Positive Aspects and Potential Downsides

Social media has both negative and positive aspects.[46]

The technological advancements we have witnessed these past decades have made social media an almost inseparable element contributing to how well we fit into society. Irrespective of this fact, the continuous use of these social media platforms has exposed many teenagers to several physical, social, and psychological challenges, and you must be aware of them to protect yourself.

Positive Aspects

- It's a medium for entertainment and gives room for self-expression. Getting in touch with people of similar interests worldwide on social media platforms like Instagram, Facebook, and Snapchat can greatly boost your confidence. When teenagers interact with like minds, it enhances their self-esteem as they can better express themselves.

- It can help you develop social skills. While some teenagers are extroverts, some are introverted. For the latter, social media platforms allow them to interact with others without withdrawing entirely into themselves. They develop social skills through social networking that help them communicate effectively and build long-lasting relationships.

Downsides

- It poses risks of developmental issues. When you become overly engrossed with social media, there is a high tendency to procrastinate over other essential activities and deprive yourself of sleep. This has affected many teenagers' academic performance and socialization. There are also possibilities of having health-related issues like obesity when this lifestyle is prolonged.
- It gives an unrealistic perception of body image. Nowadays, several social media users pose as influencers and promote different lifestyles and cultures. It's easy for teenagers to get influenced and detest their body image due to comparison.

For instance, the use of filters and photo editing apps that many social media users utilize creates unrealistic beauty standards that are impossible for teenagers to meet, leading to them adopting unhealthy habits to keep up with these unattainable goals.

Further, a media page that promotes the idea that only tanned and thin can be termed "beautiful" has people making drastic changes to their bodies. These ideologies cause teenagers to slide into depression and anxiety.

How Excessive Use of Social Media Can Affect Mental Health

Not knowing when to cut down on social media and take breaks can negatively affect your mental health. Here is how it all happens:

It Starts as an Addiction

Social media platforms are highly addictive. Most social media apps and content are designed to keep you glued to your phone. The excitement and pleasure you derive from interacting on these platforms increases dopamine levels. So, you'll crave being online whenever you aren't.

Too Much Reliance on External Validation

Many teenagers feel disappointed and invalidated when they don't get the desired interactions from their feeds. This could be a like on their post or a nice comment about an activity they shared on their page. Some people also start to compare the performance of their posts to that of their friends online. Unfortunately, this mindset takes over and lowers your self-esteem.

False Perceptions

Using filters on social media platforms has positive and negative effects on teenagers. While some may be concerned and flattered by their humorous qualities, many are engrossed in their abilities to create illusive effects like teeth whitening, clearing facial contours, etc. These illusions can make you have false perceptions, making you feel inadequate without these filters.

FOMO - Fear of Missing Out

Most teenagers cannot do without going online for even a minute. They are always curious about the latest trends. They feel they may be criticized for not being updated on these trends, so the fear of missing out clings to them. They are usually worried about missing out on a joke, message, or any information they could use to initiate a conversation with their peers. Being too engrossed with social media has several effects on not just your health but your core values as a person. You may experience an inability to direct your focus toward other activities. This is one of the many reasons why some teenagers don't perform well at school and procrastinate.

Tips on Maintaining a Healthy Balance with Social Media

Knowing the adverse effects of social media on your daily life, you should practice these tips to overcome them:

- Set specific time frames for social media. Limit your time on social media and allocate time for other important activities.
- Certain applications and features on your phone could help you monitor your screen time on every application you have installed. Use these features as a checklist for your social media activities. Being aware of the valuable time you may have misappropriated by scrolling through funny videos on TikTok can help you reset

and allocate strict timing to your social media activities.

- Don't just find yourself on social media by reflex. Ensure you have a specific reason for being online at that particular moment. Once you are done fulfilling that purpose, log out immediately.
- Avoid comparing yourself with other social media users. Most of these people live an elusive lifestyle, making you perceive a lie as truth. Focusing your attention on your social media goals is better than comparing your success.
- Put your phone away during bedtime. This will help you reduce social media distractions that limit your sleep time.
- Learn to live in the moment. Don't get so carried away by social media that you forget you are at a family reunion. Prioritize the real world.

Balancing your social media interaction will improve your mental health and give you an edge when relating with your peers in the real world. It will enhance your social relationships and foster a productive lifestyle.

Section 9: Empathy and Compassion Towards Others

If you have heard the phrase "survival of the fittest," you might know Darwin's work. Darwin opined that creating a prosperous community, fostering children, and transforming the human species into its current civilization requires compassion. Compassion and empathy are vital aspects of human living that aid survival. This section will address the purpose of empathy and compassion, focusing on their differences, the benefits of empathy and compassion, and actionable steps to help you develop these traits.

The Difference between Empathy and Compassion

These two terms are related and can be used interchangeably; however, they have unique meanings.

Empathy

*Empathy is the ability to relate to other people's feelings.*⁴⁷

Empathy is the ability to comprehend and share another person's feelings. It is appreciating shared experiences as humans and accepting that everyone hurts, feels fear, and suffers losses. You don't always have to have lived their experience to empathize with their pain. Empathy should naturally come into play when acknowledging what others have gone through. You can vicariously experience empathy by merely looking at a friend who lost a child and feeling that sense of loss. It takes guts to be in tune with another person's emotions. If you've ever been met with empathy from someone, you know how binding it is when you feel understood.

It is worth noting that feeling another individual's pain does not equate to taking it away. You need to be very careful how you make room for the painful experiences of others because they can trigger you to relive your own painful experience – which happens most of the time.

Compassion

Compassion revolves more around the state of togetherness. Compassion is bearing the weight of someone's suffering, wanting to relieve them of their pain. Though the *ideology* of compassion and empathy are the same, *they don't mean the same thing.* Empathy speaks of your ability to see and relate to the emotions of another; compassion combines those thoughts and feelings with the desire to alleviate them. Compassion is action-driven. It is the capacity and readiness to stand with the sufferer, taking on their fight.

Benefits of Empathy and Compassion

Being able to show empathy and compassion towards others has so many benefits. Here are some of them:

Improved Relationships

Empathy and compassion are vital for developing and improving strong, supportive relationships. A connection is formed every time you tune into another individual's emotional experience and offer a helping hand. Over time, your relationships will have developed a deep connectedness because of what you have endured together.

Reduced Conflicts

A bitter argument with a friend, neighbor, or colleague can be reduced if you show empathy and compassion. When you can relate and see things from their perspective, you might not be too quick to be critical or harsh with your words. Understanding this concept will change how you deal with others, making them less likely to get defensive in an argument because they know you aren't trying to "win" - you're on the same side trying to resolve the conflict together.

Personal Fulfillment

Imagine reaching out to a friend who is down and showing them kindness. You will be met with gratitude that enhances your own happiness. Being kind to others is kindness to yourself. It improves your mental and physical well-being, builds a resilient immune system, and creates a sense of fulfillment that can only be earned when you give - not just take. It is a known fact giving to others creates energy around you that ensures you get happiness back.

Actionable Steps and Exercises to Help Teenagers Develop Empathy and Compassion

Empathy and compassion are half innate and half taught. Teenagers can develop these qualities by:

Active Listening

Active listening is being aware of a person's nonverbal communication. [48]

Active listening is not distracting, shaming, judging, commanding, analyzing, or blaming the other person for the misfortune they are experiencing. Active listening is seeing and hearing beyond words, being aware of the other person's nonverbal communication, like their voice tone, talking speed, the context they are speaking from, and body language. Active listening entails adjusting to the other person's point of view and understanding their frame of reference. You must be able to tell the difference between "me" and "you" by stepping out of your internal frame of reference and learning to see it from there.

Here are exercises to help you listen actively:

- Encourage the other person to speak
- Don't be in a hurry to speak, wait
- Give them room to guide the conversation
- Accept the emotion they are feeling
- Be conscious of their body language
- Create a comfortable atmosphere for sharing

Perspective-Taking

Developing empathy and compassion helps you see, feel, and accept the perspectives of others. You try to understand their state of mind as they deal with the situation. When you take in the perspectives of others, you'll be able to see where they're coming from.

Consider the following example of perspective-taking:

Imagine you were asked to describe your friends, and you go, "Susan has a broken arm, and Cassey does not." You could see that you only viewed your friends in terms of their physicality rather than seeing them as smart, intelligent human beings. Good perspective-taking is "Susan is a smart, lovable person who always makes me laugh and helps me. I am glad I was paired with her for our geometry test because she is one of the best math wizzes in my school." You can see that your focus was on Susan's interests and what made her stand out. You're willing to see and welcome Susan's viewpoint. Always imagine how it would feel if others failed to understand your perspective.

Engaging in Acts of Kindness

Simple acts of compassion and kindness towards others in challenging times can mean so much to someone going through a tough time. You can volunteer to help others with their challenges. Helping others enhances your mental and physical well-being. Some examples/exercises for engaging in acts of kindness include:

- **Donating to a charity store:** Go through the things you haven't used for some time or don't require anymore and give them away.
- **Post a sticky note:** You can put a sticky note with an uplifting message in a public place or at your school.
- **Pay it forward:** Treat your friends or neighbors to soda, coffee, or a snack.

Empathy and compassion are worth developing because they enable you to understand, relate, and connect with others on a different level. It is fundamental to building meaningful relationships and a strong community. You become emotionally sound with enhanced communication skills when cultivating these qualities. So, as you go about your day, learn to be empathetic and compassionate towards those that come your way today.

Section 10: Your Emotional Toolkit - A Personalized Plan

Having an emotional toolkit as a teenager will help and guide you through trial and error. In this section, you'll be provided with a personalized emotional toolkit. This toolkit is a comprehensive guide designed to support and promote your psychological and emotional well-being. It offers plans and techniques that address your specific needs mentally.

The aim of going through this process is to raise your self-awareness about your triggers and how you can consciously handle them without causing any harm to you and others. Each session provides you with a framework comprising different activities and exercises you can engage in yourself and with others. Each strategy mentioned in this section can be adjusted or combined with others to meet your specific needs.

Custom Personalized Template for Every Kind of Teen

Creating a personalized kit is complex, as these activities may not fit your temperament. If any of these apply to you, feel free to put them to work. If they're not as effective or you think you have two or more of these personalities, you can also combine exercises. These activities and exercises have been discussed in detail in previous sections; go over the previous sections when applying one of these methods.

For the "Shy" Teen

Shy teens like being in their own space. [49]

As an introverted teen, you have something unique that the world doesn't know about. You do not need to compromise who you are just to be accepted by everyone else. You may often find fulfillment while refueling in quietness, but that doesn't make you a loner. You're not being weird or wrong when you feel this way, and it's okay for everyone else to misunderstand you on many occasions. You can express yourself through art, music, writing, and singing.

Are you an introverted teenager? Do you like to be in your own space and crave the need to escape the crowd? If so, you might find it hard to express yourself when you feel stressed and anxious about certain things because you feel "they wouldn't understand me if I tried." Here's a toolkit just for you:

- Start with solo mindfulness exercises. For example, deep breathing and guided meditation help build your confidence.
- Proceed into journaling. There's no better way to express yourself as an introvert than journaling your thoughts.
- Try a group mindfulness session with a few of your close friends. It's likely that your friends are also learning to process their emotions – it's a "teen" thing.

For the "Outgoing" Teen

Being an extrovert means that you often desire to be in social gatherings, and when you get hints of feeling left out, you begin suffering from FOMO (Fear Of Missing Out). You tend to be swift in those decisions that lead to self-gratification because they make you feel fulfilled and happy. Social interactions may be where you derive your energy from.

If you're that teen with an extroverted personality, then this set of activities is for you:

- Practice mindful walking, sports, and exercises to keep you active and release those endorphins to kill your stress hormones.
- Try group mindfulness workshop activities, as this resonates with your nature. You can share your experiences with trusted friends and encourage them to share theirs. This would promote positive feedback from them.

For the "Jealous" Teen

Every teen at one point in their lives experienced a form of jealousy. It's okay to feel this way sometimes. You may fight over shared interests and have bad thoughts about those you feel threatened by. It's good that you're embracing your mistakes (and reading this section!). You have to learn to check those that hold great influence over you, learn to accept rejection, and focus on your passion as a form of distraction from your feelings.

You cannot stop here, though; you have to take conscious steps towards change, and by that, you can try out mindful techniques to help you better understand your feelings. Remember that the best way to deal with your emotions is first to acknowledge that they're real. Self-awareness is very important here! Here's a guide for dealing with your emotions:

- Identify and acknowledge those negative emotions you feel are related to jealousy.
- Practice self-compassion. You need to remove those self-criticizing thoughts; they are harmful to you and others.
- Practice gratitude journaling. Shift attention from your feelings at specific times and write what you're grateful for. This can be in regard to your health, family members' health, some good news you received, a favor someone did for you, etc.

For the "Perfectionist" Teen

When you're a perfectionist, you live on high expectations that may push you to fall into depression. You don't have to get it right all the time because nothing can ever truly be perfect. Putting pressure on yourself can lead to you procrastinating most of the time.

Perfectionism can greatly contribute to anxiety, especially when your expectations are not met. Do not burden yourself with unrealistic expectations because you may have severe anxiety from not meeting them.

Here is a helpful exercise when you become restless with perfectionism:

- Practice mindfulness that helps you focus on present moments instead of your mistakes; for example, singing or listening to music, art, and creative activities. Try drawing or listening to podcasts encouraging self-worth, embracing your flaws, and using them to become inspired.

Reflecting on Which Strategies Resonate Well with You

As you read through the strategies above, decide which best applies to you. Observe your past mistakes, errors, emotional pain, and stress triggers. Ask yourself these questions to narrow down your options:

- Which mindfulness activities align with my hobbies, such as art, music, nature, dance, and so on?
- Am I comfortable practicing mindfulness with others or alone?
- Which of these strategies best soothes my common stress triggers?
- Am I very hard on myself, and do I often struggle with self-criticizing thoughts?
- What strategies can I apply to my newfound answers?

Guide to Help Build an Emotional Tool Kit

Goal Setting

When you've reflected on your emotions, you can move on to identify the areas that need work. From there, you can begin setting realistic goals for yourself. For example, if you want to reduce your anxiety during exams, set a clear goal to have a reading partner or get enough rest and set alarms for reading. You can also sing or walk around to think about what you read.

- Write down your emotional goal.

- List the emotions you want to manage:

Identify Coping Strategies

Draft strategies that align with your goals – whatever strategy you're most comfortable with or drawn to. Some coping strategies include breathing exercises, meditation, journaling, group talks, talking with a friend, or seeking professional help.

- List four exercises you can participate in to accomplish your set goal.

Establish a Support System

Take note of people who can provide you with the emotional support you need. They may be understanding friends, family members, teachers, or counselors. Share your goals, feelings, and experiences. Ask them for their support on your journey.

- Make a list of people you can confide in:

- Choose the best person from your list to help you with your current situation.

- Write down everything you want the person to know to help you communicate your feelings. This doesn't have to be done in a day; take your time to assess your feelings before putting them into writing.

While you carry out this practice, remember that you're unique, and what works for you may not work for another. As you explore and apply what makes you comfortable and in touch with yourself, remember that this is a personal journey; it takes time to adapt to change.

If you're unsure where to start, go with the easy ones, like getting a journal to write your thoughts and record your experiences and improvements. Refer back to your writing to track your journey and know when to apply more effort or celebrate an accomplishment.

Write down your triggers and apply a strategy to combat one at a time; go back and check your progress to know which ones are more effective. This is a daily practice, not a once-a-week or monthly exercise! Consistency is key to change. In this ongoing process, you will face new challenges and experiences. But you have the tools to manage whatever emotions they evoke. Most importantly, be patient with yourself and celebrate every step of the way. You should be proud of your courage to take control of your life.

A Thank You Message

To the teen who has read this book: It's been a great journey through the ten sections of this book; your engagement and dedication have been great! I want to take a moment to express my sincere gratitude to you for your commitment to your growth and emotional well-being – two things that impact you and the people around you. Your willingness to learn and apply mindful coping strategies has demonstrated your strength and resilience in overcoming life's challenges.

Your openness and willingness to build your emotional health and mindfulness are key to getting through your teenage years; as you embrace these practices now, you are laying a strong foundation for a healthy and more fulfilling life. I encourage you to continue and share these strategies with your peers and loved ones.

To the parent and caregiver of this wonderful teen: I give you my heartfelt appreciation. Your support and dedication in encouraging your teenager's well-being is truly heroic. You've done a great job fostering and creating a safe space for your child's growth. As you commit to applying the strategies from this book, be sure that the benefits outweigh any previous mistakes or struggles. Expect a positive response from your teen, and be patient with them as they begin this journey of self-discovery.

I sincerely hope the knowledge you've acquired through *Coping Skills for Teens* will positively impact your life. As I bring this to a close, I would also like to encourage you to remember that it may not always be easy and linear. Celebrate your little wins, no matter how small they are at the start. This is the beginning of your emotional growth, and I wish you all the best!

If you enjoyed this book, I'd greatly appreciate a review on Amazon because it helps me to create more books that people want. It would mean a lot to hear from you.

To leave a review:
1. Open your camera app.
2. Point your mobile device at the QR code.
3. The review page will appear in your web browser.

Thanks for your support!

Check out another book in the series

References

(N.d.-a). ApA.org. https://www.apA.org/topics/mindfulness

(N.d.-b). Research.com. https://research.com/education/student-stress-statistics

(N.d.-c). ApA.org. https://www.apA.org/topics/children/stress

(N.d.-d). Psychologicalscience.org. https://www.psychologicalscience.org/observer/dweck-growth-mindsets

Can mindfulness exercises help me? (2022, October 11). Mayo Clinic. https://www.mayocliniC.org/healthy-lifestyle/consumer-health/in-depth/mindfulness-exercises/art-20046356

Courtney E. Ackerman, M. A. (2017, February 3). 25 fun mindfulness activities for children & teens (+tips!). Positivepsychology.com. https://positivepsychology.com/mindfulness-for-children-kids-activities/

Henriksen, D., Richardson, C., & Shack, K. (2020). Mindfulness and creativity: Implications for thinking and learning. Thinking Skills and Creativity, 37 (100689), 100689. https://doi.org/10.1016/j.tsC.2020.100689

Hu, J., Zhang, J., Hu, L., Yu, H., & Xu, J. (2021). Art therapy: A complementary treatment for mental disorders. Frontiers in Psychology, 12. https://doi.org/10.3389/fpsyg.2021.686005

Koutamanis, M., Vossen, H. G. M., & Valkenburg, P. M. (2015). Adolescents' comments in social media: Why do adolescents receive negative feedback and who is most at risk? Computers in Human Behavior, 53, 486–494. https://doi.org/10.1016/j.chB.2015.07.016

Mindfulness for kids. (2020, June 11). Mindful; Mindful Communications & Such PBC. https://www.mindful.org/mindfulness-for-kids/

On, W. (2020, November 10). How does stress affect the immune system? UMMS Health. https://health.umms.org/2020/11/10/stress-immune-system/

Raypole, C. (2019, May 24). Grounding techniques: Exercises for anxiety, PTSD, and more. Healthline. https://www.healthline.com/health/grounding-techniques

Sharma, H. (2015). Meditation: Process and effects. Ayu, 36(3), 233-237. https://doi.org/10.4103/0974-8520.182756

Surzykiewicz, J., Skalski, S. B., Sołbut, A., Rutkowski, S., & Konaszewski, K. (2022). Resilience and regulation of emotions in adolescents: Serial mediation analysis through self-esteem and the perceived social support. International Journal of Environmental Research and Public Health, 19(13), 8007. https://doi.org/10.3390/ijerph19138007

Take charge of your health: A guide for teenagers. (2023, February 27). National Institute of Diabetes and Digestive and Kidney Diseases; NIDDK - National Institute of Diabetes and Digestive and Kidney Diseases. https://www.niddk.nih.gov/health-information/weight-management/take-charge-health-guide-teenagers

Tan, L., & Martin, G. (2015). Taming the adolescent mind: a randomised controlled trial examining clinical efficacy of an adolescent mindfulness-based group programme. Child and Adolescent Mental Health, 20(1), 49–55. https://doi.org/10.1111/camh.12057

(N.d.). Choosingtherapy.com. https://www.choosingtherapy.com/mindfulness-for-teens/

(N.d.). http://www.verywellmind.com/what-is-positive-thinking-2794772#toc-health-benefits-of-positive-thinking

(N.d.). Indeed.com. https://www.indeed.com/career-advice/career-development/empathic-listening

Abigail, E. (2022, May 7). Essay about Adolescence problems. GetGoodEssay; Get Good Essay. https://getgoodessay.com/college-essays/essay-about-adolescence/

Barlow, D. H., Ellard, K. K., Fairholme, C. P., Farchione, T. J., Boisseau, C. L., Allen, L. B., & Ehrenreich-May, J. (2010). Understanding your emotions. In Unified Protocol for Transdiagnostic Treatment of Emotional Disorders (pp. 53–66). Oxford University Press.

Booker, D. (2019). What is stress?: Dealing with stress. Rosen Classroom. https://www.unicef.org/parenting/mental-health/what-is-stress

Building resilience: how to bounce back from setbacks. (2021, October 18). Maxme - We Maximise Human Potential. https://www.maxme.com.au/insights/building-resilience-how-to-bounce-back-from-setbacks

Coaches, M. T. (2021, October 1). Compassion vs. empathy: What is the difference? Tonyrobbins.com. https://www.tonyrobbins.com/mind-meaning/compassion-vs-empathy/

Compassion definition. (n.d.). Greater Good. https://greatergood.berkeley.edu/topic/compassion/definition

Eatough, E. (n.d.). 15 common red flags in a relationship to look out for. Betterup.com. https://www.betterup.com/blog/red-flags-in-a-relationship

Eatough, E. (n.d.). How to deal with rejection: 7 tips. Betterup.com. https://www.betterup.com/blog/how-to-deal-with-rejection

Emotion. (n.d.). SparkNotes. https://www.sparknotes.com/psychology/psych101/emotion/section2/

Facing the challenges of adolescence. (2015, June 13). Action Health Incorporated. https://www.actionhealthinc.org/facing-the-challenges-of-adolescence/

Family conflict. (n.d.). Gov.au. https://www.betterhealth.vic.gov.au/health/healthyliving/family-conflict

gb1djk. (2019, June 19). Heads Up! A toolkit of sessions to run with young people to promote mental health & emotional well-being. Free Social Work Tools and Resources: Socialworkerstoolbox.com. https://www.socialworkerstoolbox.com/heads-toolkit-sessions-run-young-people-promote-mental-health-emotional-well

Gongala, S. (2014, November 26). 13 positive and negative influences of media on teenagers. MomJunction. https://www.momjunction.com/articles/positive-and-negative-influences-of-media-on-teenagers_00107975/

Healthy vs. Unhealthy relationships. (n.d.). WebMD. https://www.webmd.com/sex-relationships/healthy-vs-unhealthy-relationships

Here's the difference between sympathy, empathy, and compassion. (2020, January 6). Rethink Breast Cancer. https://rethinkbreastcancer.com/heres-the-difference-between-sympathy-empathy-and-compassion/

Hess, M. (2022, October 14). The impact of positivity for online school students. Connectionsacademy.com; Connections Academy. https://www.connectionsacademy.com/support/resources/article/positivity-impact-students/

How to deal with the negative effects of social media. (n.d.). Headspace. https://www.headspace.com/mindfulness/negative-effects-of-social-media

Hwang, H., & Matsumoto, D. (2019). 11.2 Functions of emotions. In Introduction to Psychology. University of Saskatchewan Open Press.

Hwang, H., & Matsumoto, D. (n.d.). Functions of emotions. Noba. https://nobaproject.com/modules/functions-of-emotions

John, A. (2018, November 24). What are the benefits and advantages of Positive thinking? Medium. https://medium.com/@likhithak.dmp/what-are-the-benefits-and-advantages-of-positive-thinking-cd46ba3154c4

Kendra Cherry, M. (2012, March 5). Benefits of positive thinking for body and mind. Verywell Mind. https://www.verywellmind.com/benefits-of-positive-thinking-2794767

Kendra Cherry, M. (2012, November 16). 5 Reasons Emotions Are Important. Verywell Mind. https://www.verywellmind.com/the-purpose-of-emotions-2795181

McLaren, K. (2013, October 29). The Six Essential Aspects of Empathy, Part 4: Perspective taking. Karla McLaren. https://karlamclaren.com/the-six-essential-aspects-of-empathy-part-4-perspective-taking/

MindTools. (n.d.). Mindtools.com. https://www.mindtools.com/ao310a2/developing-resilience

Moods: helping pre-teens and teens manage emotional ups and downs. (2022, October 20). Raising Children Network. https://raisingchildren.net.au/pre-teens/mental-health-physical-health/about-mental-health/ups-downs

MSU extension. (2015, February 2). MSU Extension. https://www.canr.msu.edu/news/mindfulness_in_adolescence

Navigating Through the Ups and Downs of Adolescence - Carolina Counseling Services - Southern Pines & Pinehurst. (2021). https://www.southernpines.carolinacounselingservices.com/navigating-through-the-ups-and-downs-of-adolescence/

No title. (n.d.). Lancastergeneralhealth.org. https://www.lancastergeneralhealth.org/health-hub-home/2021/september/the-effects-of-social-media-on-mental-health

Obot, A. (2022, July 17). 16 secrets to maintaining a good and healthy relationship with friends. Inspired Scoop. https://www.inspiredscoop.com/2022/07/16-secrets-to-maintain-good-and-healthy.html

Patterson, A. (2021, May 6). Seven ways to balance social media and mental health. Greater Phoenix Chamber. https://phoenixchamber.com/2021/05/06/seven-ways-to-balance-social-media-and-mental-health/

Persevering in the face of academic setbacks – academic success center – blog. (n.d.). Utoronto.Ca. https://blogs.studentlife.utoronto.ca/academicsuccess/persevering-in-the-face-of-academic-setbacks/

Pmp®, S. K. | . (1677579041000). Empathy: The power of understanding and connecting with others. Linkedin.com. https://www.linkedin.com/pulse/empathy-power-understanding-connecting-others-samrat-khanorkar/

Positive thinking: Stop negative self-talk to reduce stress. (2022, February 3). Mayo Clinic. https://www.mayoclinic.org/healthy-lifestyle/stress-management/in-depth/positive-thinking/art-20043950

Prajapati, M. (1595068856000). How to deal with friendship problems. Linkedin.com. https://www.linkedin.com/pulse/how-deal-friendship-problems-maitry-prajapati/

Purves, D., Augustine, G. J., Fitzpatrick, D., Katz, L. C., LaMantia, A.-S., McNamara, J. O., & Mark Williams, S. (2001). Physiological changes associated with emotion. Sinauer Associates.

Reid, S. (n.d.). Empathy: How to feel and respond to the emotions of others - Helpguide.org. https://www.helpguide.org/articles/relationships-communication/empathy.htm

Remez, S. (2020, May 27). The power of positive thinking: Learn to transform your life. Success Consciousness | Positive Thinking - Personal Development. https://www.successconsciousness.com/blog/positive-attitude/positive-thinking/

Shaver, T. K., Ozga, J. E., Zhu, B., Anderson, K. G., Martens, K. M., & Vonder Haar, C. (2019). Long-term deficits in risky decision-making after traumatic brain injury on a rat analog of the Iowa gambling task. Brain Research, 1704, 103–113. https://doi.org/10.1016/j.brainres.2018.10.004

Sincero, S. M. (n.d.). Nature of emotions. Explorable.com. https://explorable.com/nature-of-emotions

Sutton, J. (2016, July 21). Active listening: The art of empathetic conversation. Positivepsychology.com. https://positivepsychology.com/active-listening/

The 14 most important characteristics of healthy relationships. (2016, June 10). Mindbodygreen. https://www.mindbodygreen.com/articles/characteristics-of-healthy-relationships

The mental health of adolescents. (n.d.). https://www.who.int/news-room/fact-sheets/detail/adolescent-mental-health

The Oracles. (2018, December 8). "Most people probably would have stopped" – 8 tips on overcoming even the most crippling setbacks. CNBC. https://www.cnbc.com/2018/12/07/8-tips-on-overcoming-even-the-most-crippling-setbacks.html

Three things positive thinking is NOT. (n.d.). Forgoodness-sake.com. https://forgoodness-sake.com/three-things-positive-thinking-is-not/

UWA. (2019, June 27). The science of emotion: Exploring the basics of emotional psychology. UWA Online. https://online.uwa.edu/news/emotional-psychology/

VISIONS. (2022, April 19). 4 causes of teenage stress. Visions Treatment Centers. https://visionsteen.com/4-causes-of-teenage-stress/?amp

Image Sources

[1] https://unsplash.com/photos/ljoCgjs63SM?utm_source=unsplash&utm_medium=referral&utm_content=creditShareLink

[2] https://www.pexels.com/photo/photo-of-yawning-man-with-his-hands-up-and-eyes-closed-sitting-at-a-table-with-his-laptop-3760538/

[3] https://www.pexels.com/photo/people-inside-room-12312/

[4] https://www.pexels.com/photo/woman-in-white-coat-blowing-bubbles-5849026/

[5] https://unsplash.com/photos/xcvXS6wDCAY?utm_source=unsplash&utm_medium=referral&utm_content=creditShareLink

[6] https://unsplash.com/photos/4p0C_OiXNiM?utm_source=unsplash&utm_medium=referral&utm_content=creditShareLink

[7] https://unsplash.com/photos/MlhJNEUQpBs?utm_source=unsplash&utm_medium=referral&utm_content=creditShareLink

[8] https://unsplash.com/photos/Av7Nkvc49ag?utm_source=unsplash&utm_medium=referral&utm_content=creditShareLink

[9] https://unsplash.com/photos/StdafGIT520?utm_source=unsplash&utm_medium=referral&utm_content=creditShareLink

[10] https://unsplash.com/photos/fOS2IMOzsDA?utm_source=unsplash&utm_medium=referral&utm_content=creditShareLink

[11] https://unsplash.com/photos/v9bnfMCvKbg?utm_source=unsplash&utm_medium=referral&utm_content=creditShareLink

[12] https://unsplash.com/photos/jYzIgpgWgPo?utm_source=unsplash&utm_medium=referral&utm_content=creditShareLink

[13] https://unsplash.com/photos/xmddEHvCisc?utm_source=unsplash&utm_medium=referral&utm_content=creditShareLink

[14] https://unsplash.com/photos/4qnhBQv4qcg?utm_source=unsplash&utm_medium=referral&utm_content=creditShareLink

[15] https://unsplash.com/photos/bbjmFMdWYfw?utm_source=unsplash&utm_medium=referral&utm_content=creditShareLink

[16] https://www.pexels.com/photo/scrapbook-on-white-textile-3115623/

[17] https://www.pexels.com/photo/photo-of-woman-wearing-beige-jumpsuit-3120864/

[18] https://unsplash.com/photos/M6dAnUgiOlQ?utm_source=unsplash&utm_medium=referral&utm_content=creditShareLink

[19] https://unsplash.com/photos/CqX6IhVj2TI?utm_source=unsplash&utm_medium=referral&utm_content=creditShareLink

[20] https://www.pexels.com/photo/man-doing-jump-shot-1905009/

[21] https://www.pexels.com/photo/group-of-friends-singing-while-sitting-on-beach-sand-7149158/

[22] https://unsplash.com/photos/7GPnPHRksDE?utm_source=unsplash&utm_medium=referral&utm_content=creditShareLink

[23] https://www.pexels.com/photo/close-up-shot-of-a-person-holding-a-green-beaded-necklace-8164518/

[24] https://www.pexels.com/photo/photo-of-women-stretching-together-4056723/

[25] https://unsplash.com/photos/khewjv5l4Zo?utm_source=unsplash&utm_medium=referral&utm_content=creditShareLink

[26] https://unsplash.com/photos/sp-p7uuT0tw?utm_source=unsplash&utm_medium=referral&utm_content=creditShareLink

[27] https://www.pexels.com/photo/a-bacon-and-egg-sandwich-over-a-wooden-box-6529599/

[28] https://unsplash.com/photos/mrY3CX8kL0w?utm_source=unsplash&utm_medium=referral&utm_content=creditShareLink

[29] https://unsplash.com/photos/QJssnBZfqmQ?utm_source=unsplash&utm_medium=referral&utm_content=creditShareLink

[30] https://unsplash.com/photos/R4sP8_Bq0Bw?utm_source=unsplash&utm_medium=referral&utm_content=creditShareLink

[31] https://unsplash.com/photos/zNRITe8NPqY?utm_source=unsplash&utm_medium=referral&utm_content=creditShareLink

[32] https://unsplash.com/photos/jqxB3C0YNG0?utm_source=unsplash&utm_medium=referral&utm_content=creditShareLink

[33] https://unsplash.com/photos/Cs3v8Mn6-Gk?utm_source=unsplash&utm_medium=referral&utm_content=creditShareLink

[34] https://unsplash.com/photos/3cAMUE3YAO8?utm_source=unsplash&utm_medium=referral&utm_content=creditShareLink

[35] https://unsplash.com/photos/5IHz5WhosQE?utm_source=unsplash&utm_medium=referral&utm_content=creditShareLink

[36] https://unsplash.com/photos/n8L1VYaypcw?utm_source=unsplash&utm_medium=referral&utm_content=creditShareLink

[37] https://unsplash.com/photos/333oj7zFsdg?utm_source=unsplash&utm_medium=referral&utm_content=creditShareLink

[38] https://unsplash.com/photos/sLp-kPZatLc?utm_source=unsplash&utm_medium=referral&utm_content=creditShareLink

[39] https://unsplash.com/photos/ABUWC-0a7_A?utm_source=unsplash&utm_medium=referral&utm_content=creditShareLink

[40] https://unsplash.com/photos/uxEH3TufYNU?utm_source=unsplash&utm_medium=referral&utm_content=creditShareLink

[41] https://unsplash.com/photos/sxQz2VfoFBE?utm_source=unsplash&utm_medium=referral&utm_content=creditShareLink

[42] https://unsplash.com/photos/NGxd0beBLps?utm_source=unsplash&utm_medium=referral&utm_content=creditShareLink

[43] https://unsplash.com/photos/4lA1sDFr8Y8?utm_source=unsplash&utm_medium=referral&utm_content=creditShareLink

[44] https://unsplash.com/photos/4le7k9XVYjE?utm_source=unsplash&utm_medium=referral&utm_content=creditShareLink

[45] https://unsplash.com/photos/-uHVRvDr7pg?utm_source=unsplash&utm_medium=referral&utm_content=creditShareLink

[46] https://unsplash.com/photos/mr4JG4SYOF8?utm_source=unsplash&utm_medium=referral&utm_content=creditShareLink

[47] https://unsplash.com/photos/KQfxVDHGCUg?utm_source=unsplash&utm_medium=referral&utm_content=creditShareLink

[48] https://unsplash.com/photos/Sp1uQo368fA?utm_source=unsplash&utm_medium=referral&utm_content=creditShareLink

[49] https://unsplash.com/photos/NQTphr4Pr60?utm_source=unsplash&utm_medium=referral&utm_content=creditShareLink